Bull Sh*t
with Cream on It

A Leadership Memoir

by

Linda F. Robertson

DORRANCE
PUBLISHING CO
EST. 1920
PITTSBURGH, PENNSYLVANIA 15238

Dorrance Publishing Co
585 Alpha Drive
Pittsburgh, PA 15238
Visit our website at *www.dorrancebookstore.com*

ISBN: 979-8-8868-3260-0
eISBN: 979-8-8868-3656-1

To my parents,
Dot and Lee Brunk.

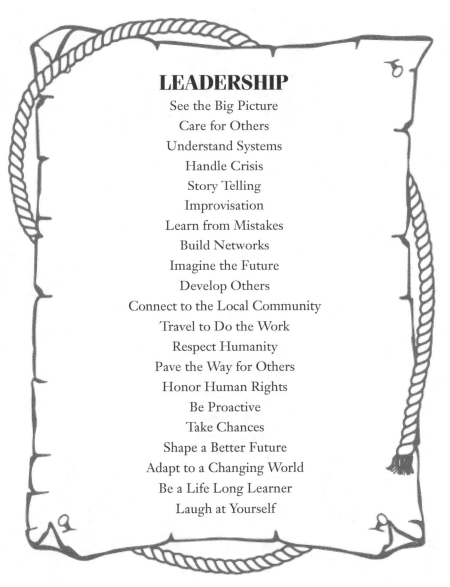

LEADERSHIP

See the Big Picture
Care for Others
Understand Systems
Handle Crisis
Story Telling
Improvisation
Learn from Mistakes
Build Networks
Imagine the Future
Develop Others
Connect to the Local Community
Travel to Do the Work
Respect Humanity
Pave the Way for Others
Honor Human Rights
Be Proactive
Take Chances
Shape a Better Future
Adapt to a Changing World
Be a Life Long Learner
Laugh at Yourself

This story of stories ropes together these
Leadership Tools, Skills, and Musts!

Chapter One:

Storm of the Century

"Expect accumulation of 35 inches of snow, and wind gusts as high as 40 miles per hour. Temperature will plummet to 10 degrees below zero."

Tuned to KWOR, 1340 AM, the radio announcer's voice warned of what was coming. All the ranchers in Wyoming were glued to the weather reports in those days. This wasn't the first big snow storm of the winter of 1949. A record-breaking blizzard kicked off the new year in the southern part of the state.

Here at Leora's, snow piled high all around the house. The wind howled. Flakes blew in under the front door and melted on the floor. Frost formed magical patterns of snowflakes on the kitchen window.

More snow? I was too young to understand all the ramifications, but the look on Mom's face shouted concern.

Dad had taken on new responsibilities in the livestock business, and 1949 was not the best winter to be a new rancher. Just a few months ago, Dad and Mom signed the lease of the Leora Hillberry Ranch on Gooseberry Creek in Hot Springs County, Wyoming. Over 1000 ewes were in the lambing sheds across the gulch and down the hill from our little house. My sister Nancy, a first grader, was boarding with Aunt Vera to go to school in Grass Creek. Born during World War II, when Dad was in the Army in the Pacific Theatre, Nancy had spent the first two years of her life alone with Mom at our grandparents' homes. They had grown very close. I wondered if Mom was worried about Nancy being away from her during such a storm.

"Jackson Hole is isolated with 14 days of snow! Route 16 and Powder River Pass are closed. Route 20 to Cody is closed due to high winds and blowing snow. Travel is dangerous everywhere." The news on the radio wasn't making Mom feel any better.

Before we moved into this two-room ranch house, Mom evicted the mice. She scrubbed and sanitized for a week before she thought the house was clean enough for her family. Blowing slightly in the puffs of wind coming through the sill, white lace curtains hung at the window. The large dining table that dominated the room had a flowery new tablecloth. Mom, petite and purposeful, added more coal on the fire in the cast iron cook stove that graced the corner of the kitchen of the two-room ranch house. She turned her attention to peeling potatoes for the lambing crew who would be coming in soon.

Although I was just three years old, I knew enough not to ask her to play with me. I sat at the table and was busy with the coloring book that had been one of Grandma Schweighart's Christmas gifts. New crayons, perfect in their shape, have a waxy smell to be enjoyed. The new oil tablecloth also had a waxy paraffin aroma. In the simplicity of our environment, I was learning to notice the littlest things.

On the radio, Tennessee Ernie Ford belted out "Clippity clop, clippity clop along, Muuuuuule Train." At least the music following the weather report made us feel better. The Hillberry Ranch didn't need a mule train to bring in supplies, but it was definitely isolated.

This remote ranch was tucked up against the Hillberry Rim in a corner of Hot Springs County.

To the north of the ranch, Bobcat Draw Badlands Wilderness Study Area, covering 19,540 acres, is a natural geological barrier. In addition, the U.S. National Park Service protected more lands, the Gooseberry Badlands and the Fifteen Mile Wild Horse Herd Management Area. (Dad used to skip school, and run wild horses there!) The U.S. Department of Interior's description of this area lists *solitude* as one of its features. Even today, the National Park Service's Gooseberry Badlands Trail Sign warns hikers to take water and to beware of rattlesnakes. The towns of Worland and Thermopolis were over 40 miles away. You had to drive nearly 20 miles to get to Grass Creek, a Standard Oil of Ohio company town, and Meeteetse, a ranching community. Yes, *solitude* was easy to find at Leora's.

Dad and Mom had just taken a three-year lease from Leora Hillberry. Her husband, George, had died suddenly from Rocky Mountain spotted tick fever. George Hillberry was a true sheep man. He tended his own sheep in the mountains in the summer until his family grew too big to live in a sheep wagon for three summer months. He built lambing and shearing sheds when other ranchers in the area did not enjoy this luxury.

His untimely death meant that his young widow had to find someone to manage the ranch. Leora and the four boys lived in Worland so the boys could go to school. But in searching for someone to lease the ranch, Leora had difficulty. Most interested prospective ranchers said no—1000 sheep was too small to be profitable. Other ranches had more sheep. Grandpa Schweighart, over on Cottonwood Creek, had two bands of 1000 each. The LU Ranch, up Grass Creek, had over 3500 sheep. Most prospective rancher wives rejected the two-room house that hadn't been lived in for years. Who would want a two-room house for their family? Other prospective ranching families said no because of the concern about education for their children. School bus transportation was not provided for children living this far away from schools in Hot Springs County.

Dad grew up further downriver on Gooseberry Creek and knew what it took to make a living on a Wyoming ranch. Maybe 1000 head of sheep was too small, but Dad also had a small herd of cattle that he owned. The addition of the cattle could make this opportunity profitable. In the three years after coming home from the Army, he worked hard and focused on the future by buying and breeding a small herd. Seeing an opportunity for his young family, Dad also wanted to "work for himself."

Dad, who always wore a hat to protect his fair skin from the harsh Wyoming weather, looked the image of a cowboy, with shoulders wide enough for big responsibilities, narrow hips, and a big grin. He wore Lee jeans with the leather logo in the back as a belt hoop—his name was Lee so we thought that was just perfect. Now a blizzard was threatening the profitability of his new enterprise.

As the wind continued to creep through the window sill, I shivered and turned my attention back to the radio. Another popular ballad followed, "An old cowboy went riding out one dark and windy day…" I looked out the window—it was dark and windy here, too.

When Marty Robbins came to the chorus of "Yippee-Yi-o, Yippie-Yi Yay, Ghost Riders in the Sky," Mom sang along. I think she was trying not to focus on the snow and wind.

Bubbling boiling potatoes and sizzling frying meat warmed the room. Well, they warmed the room until Dad and three men from the lambing crew opened the door. Old Man Winter rushed in ahead of them, piling snow on the floor and brushing my cheeks with cold. Stomping their feet to rid boots of snow and ice, they removed their layers of overshoes, coats, scarves, and gloves. I saw that some had two shirts on, too. Each man drank heavily from the water bucket's ladle as they took turns washing up.

Mom dished up chicken fried steaks, potatoes, gravy, corn, Jell-o salad, and pies. I put away my crayons and coloring book, and sat at my place at the table.

Cold and hungry men spooned mashed potatoes and milk gravy on their plates in silence. Hot food—and plenty of it—had their attention. As stomachs calmed and shoulders warmed, a serious discussion of the storm began.

"When will this snow ever quit?"

"I have never seen this much snow in one winter. And the wind, will it ever stop?"

"Why did so many lambs choose today to be born?"

"Is there some way we can build wind breaks to keep snow out of the sheds?"

"Are we ever going to sleep again?" This rocket blast of questions came from the crew members who were working 15–18-hour shifts.

Dad's face was serious as the talk turned to solving the problems brought about by the storm. Mom, always neat and tidy, began to offer apple pie and coffee to the crew as these big-picture decisions were hashed out.

"We could run electric lines from the pole by the barn to the sheds. Bring all the cords that you can find, and the trouble lamps from the machine shed.

The trouble lights will provide some heat for the newly born lambs for the first hours of their lives," Fred suggested.

We did have electricity, thanks to a cooperative, Hot Springs Rural Electric Association. Area ranchers put together the Hot Springs REA to bring electricity from Boysen hydroelectric dam on the Wind River. Dad was a new active member.

"Yes, that's a good idea. Will you work on that? We could also use irrigation canvases, and nail them to the wooden railings to block the wind and snow. Uppy, you know where the hammer and nails are. Start that right away." Dad did not want to waste any time.

"Lee, you are lucky to have lambing sheds. Think of the ranchers who are range lambing!"

Dad was not sure that he was lucky right now. "Let's move bales of hay to the edges of the corrals to block the snow and wind. I'll take the wagon and load up some bales."

I did not know then but now realize, that those conversations at this big table in the small house in a remote Wyoming sheep and cattle ranch were the beginning of my leadership training. Dad and Mom were providing a Leadership Pre-School experience for me without knowing it. As you will see, my experiences growing up in this remote location provided a rich laboratory for leadership training—not be found in the best of early childhood formal institutions. This memoir will tell of my early years—3-8, and how the unique experiences helped me lead public schools and global university centers until the ripe old age of 74.

At this kitchen table—or we might say today, home office—discussions of an uncertain future were served with venison steak, boiled potatoes, and gravy. A well-balanced meal and lots of talk provided both body and language nutrition for me as a toddler. In addition to the value of good meals and rich discussion, these conversations provided the opportunity to see the big picture, an important leadership ability. It came daily, abundant in quality and quantity, and peppered with laughter, news, and problem solving. As an educator now, I know that this rich language exposure is the foundation that helps build future literacy, achievement, and also develops dispositions for leadership.

Today the storm might be the center of the conversation, but on another less urgent day our kitchen might be filled with laughter. Like the night that Uppy Schyrak, then a new hired hand, spooned Mom's famous nutmeg sauce (meant for the freshly baked white cake) on his potatoes. He thought it was gravy. We all laughed and kidded him about it.

Another day the news on the radio might lead to thoughts on the war in Korea. I was at the table for all of that. Brain patterns were being developed for seeing the big picture.

SEE THE BIG PICTURE: A LEADERSHIP MUST

Wyoming Historian Dr. Grace Raymond Herbard
says about Chief Washakie,
*Though born and reared a nomad and doubtless
a passionate love of the free life of the wilds,
he had the wisdom to see that the old days were doomed.*
From *Washakie: Sixty Years an Unchallenged Chief*, 1995.

But today Dad's mind was not on designing leadership training for his young daughter. A big puff of wind was felt through the door frame and window sill. Dad was thinking of the lambs and the storm. His attention was on the bottom line—lambs were a cash crop. We needed every lamb to survive to make a profit. The storm had to be met head on! Dad and the men put on their heavy coats, overshoes, gloves, scarves, and hats. The cold rush of wind and snow swept in across the kitchen as they opened the door and disappeared in the blinding snow.

Mom and I were alone in the kitchen, clearing dishes, and getting me ready for bed, when suddenly Dad appeared at the door again. This time he had a newborn lamb in his arms. He growled, "Dot, get some towels and boxes. Too many lambs are being born tonight. The heat lamps are not strong enough. We will bring them here by the kitchen stove."

As an afterthought, he added, "Just until they gain strength…." He was remembering how hard Mom had worked at cleaning the house so we could move in! Mom wouldn't even allow Tippy, the sheep dog, to come into the house.

Mom found a box for it in the pantry, and put towels and newspapers on the floor under the box. The little lamb was so weak. I sat next to its box, pulling the towel over it like you would tuck a baby under a blanket. Mom prepared a bottle to try to feed it. We could hear the wind howling.

Before we knew it, Uppy burst in the door, spreading snow over the floor. His arms were full—two more lambs. "Oh, no!" Mom exclaimed, "More?" Uppy laid the two lambs on the newspapers near the box, and rushed back out into the night.

As he disappeared behind the closing door, we could just barely hear him say, "There will be more." The wind blew his words away.

In a short time, it was not one lamb in the kitchen, but 5. . .then 10. . . then 15 . . .and finally as many as 20 lambs were in boxes, lying on towels, and running around the kitchen! The snow and wind continued. When would it stop? How many ewes and lambs would die? We all were concerned. I think I was the only one who went to bed that night.

As I was drifting off to sleep, I wondered, "Was this blizzard going to be like the New Year's Day blizzard?"

The big blizzard in the southern part of the state in early January filled the airwaves on the radio for days. Winds blew up to 80 miles per hour. Snow, swept by the wind, made drifts 20 to 30 feet high. Whole towns were completely shut off from outside supplies for weeks. Trains on the Union Pacific railroad in the southern part of the state were stalled because of the snow. No trains meant university basketball teams on the way to tournaments in Utah were stranded in small towns along the way. News reports told of the airdrops of hay to hungry cattle. Thousands of cattle and sheep had piled up against fences in drifts and were found dead. Yes, Uppy had been right the other night at the dinner table when he said that Dad was lucky that we had lambing sheds near the house.

When I jumped out of bed the next morning, I heard the bleating of many lambs. I opened the door to the kitchen, and peeked in. There was Mom trying

7

her best to keep the lambs in the boxes. As the lambs gained strength, they climbed out and bleated noisily. Lambs were also using the newspapers to "do their business," as Mom called it. This did not make Mom happy.

Later that morning after breakfast was over and the dishes washed, Dad came in to see if any lambs were strong enough to be taken back to their mothers. Mom was delighted to see the number of lambs start to dwindle. She had to cook for the lambing crew, but she had been so busy with keeping lambs in the boxes, and wiping up "their business" that she hadn't even thought about lunch.

Dad took two of the lambs with him as he went out the door. Mom sighed, "I guess the men will have to do with hamburger gravy over bread today for lunch. That is all that I have time to make."

At noon, some of the men came in with good news and less snow to track all over the floor for Mom. The blizzard was letting up a little. At least the wind was stopping. This meant that the heat lamps in the sheds were warm enough for the newborns. No one had their arms full of newborn lambs to add to those by the kitchen stove. No one complained about hamburger gravy over thick slices of Mom's good homemade bread. Always resourceful, Mom had opened some delicious home-canned peaches to go with the simple meal. With her homemade chocolate chip cookies as a treat, the men sat in silence and ate in a hurry. They were dead tired.

Wearily, the lucky men who were the first to eat, put on their coats, over-shoes, gloves, and hats. And then came the best sign of all that the storm was lessening. Each man took a lamb or two with him. Soon the last of the lambing crew came to the house for hamburger gravy. They also left with lambs in their arms. As Mom was mopping up the area around the stove where so many lambs had been, she looked at the one lamb left in the box.

"Well, my dear, it is just you and me now!"

She wasn't talking to me. Maybe she was warming up to having lambs in the house.

"Well, I better do these dishes, and think what to cook for supper. It better be good, since I just gave them hamburger gravy for lunch."

I think she was talking more to herself than to me. I went over to play with the last lamb. I was going to miss the excitement of having lambs in the house.

I enjoyed the snow as Mom snapped this photo documenting the height of the drifts in front of the Ford Tractor tire. This was a measurement everyone knew.
Family Photo.

On the third day, the sun came out. With help from Mom, I struggled into my snow suit and boots, and went outside to explore. I was shocked to see the hay wagon piled high with dead lambs and ewes. Wow! That many died! I stood there for a minute just looking. No wonder Dad's shoulders were sagging yesterday.

I called to Tippy, "Let's go see the lambs." It was comforting to have the dog with me.

Tippy and I ventured down to the sheep sheds, and found that many ewes were adopting newborn, orphaned lambs. Ewes claim their lambs by smell. If a lamb died at birth, Dad and the hired men would quickly skin the dead lamb. The wool and skin was then draped over an orphaned lamb. It was important to have the lamb adopted so that he or she did not have to be bottle-fed all summer.

I climbed the railings, and studied intently the reengineering of the lambing sheds before me. The corrals were transformed. Ewes and lambs were thriving. Dad and the men had worked miracles. The number of electric cords, lamps, bales of hay, and canvas shelters amazed me. I watched the men work with each lamb as it was born, urging it to get up and nurse. I saw the tired men tenderly push together the new lamb and birthing ewe. Watching the men working in the lambing sheds, I could see that their actions saved so many.

The evidence of death was piled high in the hay wagon—a white mound not unlike the huge snow drifts all around the sheds and barns. How would these losses affect the finances in the fall? Income from selling lambs was a big part in the success or failure of ranching. Yes, Dad was concerned, but he also had to take care of the ewes and lambs bleating noisily before me in the lambing sheds and pens. His decisions had saved them. In front of me were scores of new lambs bleating, nursing, sleeping, and enjoying the heat of the sun. What I was seeing was a valuable leadership lesson which could be called, "taking care of the flock."

CARE FOR OTHERS—A LEADERSHIP MUST

*In time of crisis people want to know you care,
more than they care what you know.*
—Will Rogers

With the snow storm over, Dad caught his breath. His attention turned to the cows in the open range.

"Uppy and Fred, you keep your eyes on things here. I am going to check the cattle."

Dad saddled up Bay, his most reliable horse. He put panyards filled with cottonseed cakes on the pack mule and headed out to check on the cattle. Tippy trailed behind the mule—sort of making a mule train, I thought. As Dad rode out of sight, I hoped our cows were not piled up against a fence in the snow. I remembered the radio telling of the January blizzard, and airplanes dropping hay to the cattle.

I ran to the house, and burst in asking, "Mom, Dad is taking just cotton-seed cake to his cattle. Will the National Guard come in an airplane and drop hay to our cattle, too?" I was worried, too.

"No, Linda." Mom was reassuring both me and herself, "I am sure that our cattle found a draw to get out of the wind and blowing snow. We are sort of on a higher plateau than some of the ranches. That should help." Our ranch elevation was around 5000 feet.

And then another thought entered her head: "Although maybe not. Nothing survives in the badlands."

Luckily for us, the old Wyoming wind had swept snow away in some areas, allowing the cattle to graze for food among the sage brush and greasewood bushes. Our cattle did survive. But before Dad could take them hay, he needed to do something with the hay wagon's current load—dead lambs and ewes. The cows were pregnant with the calves for next fall's crop. We wanted big, healthy calves and that meant that the cows needed to eat.

When the sheep and cattle were taken care of Dad said, "I need to go check on Cottonseed Jack."

Cottonseed Jack lived on a 160-acre plot of land further up Gooseberry Creek than we were. He lived in a sheep wagon, looking lonely in the middle of the sage brush hills. Because he didn't have alfalfa hay fields or mountain ranges for his few cattle, he fed them cottonseed cakes year-round. Thus he was known as Cottonseed Jack. He was basically a recluse, but would occasionally come to area ranches for a meal. I was always a bit scared of him, but Dad and Mom treated him like everyone else who sat at our table. Mom and Dad were setting an example that each living being—orphaned lambs, grazing cows, or exotic neighbors—should be treated with dignity and to offer them help when needed.

Leora's Ranch was a leadership preschool for me in that first winter of 1949. As I mentioned before, the experiences at Leora's Ranch and the early years of my life would form the dispositions for leadership that would serve me well in the administrative positions that I held in public schools and at Kent State University in Ohio.

In the schools and university, "taking care of the flock" may look different than the view of the sheds on the Leora's Ranch, but the disposition for a caring leadership style was born in seeing results in a life-threatening situation.

As a high school principal years later, it seemed natural for me to "care for the flock" in many ways. One story stands out. Aurora High School serves a predominately white suburb of Aurora, near Cleveland, Ohio. We had only a few African American students. One African American couple who owned a store in a predominately black suburb had lived in Aurora for all twelve years of their son's schooling. But in his senior year, this black student withdraw from Aurora High School as his family was moving closer to his father's store. He was sad about leaving the only school he had ever known. We said goodbye, and he left to enroll in the other school. Two days later, I saw him at McDonald's in Aurora as I was returning from the school board's administrative offices.

I stopped and asked him, "Why aren't you in school?"

He answered, "I went to school for a few days. I was too white to fit in. I won't go back."

"Too white? What did you mean?" I inquired.

"I have lived in Aurora all my life. I am not black enough to survive that school."

He wasn't going back. He wasn't going to finish his senior year. Like Dad cared for lambs and Cottonseed Jack, I knew I had to care for this student, even if he was no longer a legal resident of the school district that I served. He was 18—the legal age to drop out of school. But I just couldn't leave him there.

Because he was 18 and no longer a minor, he could become a resident of Aurora and then return to Aurora High School with the legal status of an emancipated minor. But he did need an Aurora address, and an income to show he was independent from his parents. Luckily, he was in a special vocational program where his senior year was at an employment site. So he already had an income. We found a room where he could pay rent, and he then met all the legal requirements to go to school in Aurora. Once again, an eager student, he returned to Aurora High School. When he graduated in May, his parents expressed their deep appreciation. Empathy and concern for others is a skill needed for leaders. The Aurora community had entrusted me with their students. It was my responsibility to make sure that they all succeeded. Dad's favorite cowboy philosopher, Will

Rogers, reminds us to care for others through his understated wisdom: *In time of crisis people want to know that you care, more than they care what you know.*

The experience at the kitchen table discussions also was a gift in terms of seeing the big picture, a leadership responsibility. I was not only having a child's experience at Leora's, I was privileged to be part of the decision making, the visioning for the future, and of shaping what that future might look like. This leadership disposition of seeing the big picture served me well as I took on the responsibilities of being the Director of the Gerald H. Read Center for International and Intercultural Education at Kent State University in my second career. The previous director had only been part time, and the Read Center was mostly known for its educational travel program and hosting one or two big name lectures on campus each year. I saw a bigger potential for the Center—the Center could be a catalyst for the advancement of international and intercultural education. The key words in this mission statement set for the Center were *catalyst* and *advancement*. Gerald Read had been a catalyst for understanding the Soviet education systems by pioneering educational trips to countries behind the Iron Curtain. In the era after 9/11 and the attacks on the Twin Towers, the Read Center now focused on the Islamic world to promote intercultural understanding. My husband Darrell Robertson (Rob) was in business in Turkey, and he and his contacts in Turkey helped to open doors for the Read Center to connect with projects in Turkey. You will hear of many of these in later stories about the Turkish Women's Leadership Project, Euphrates Tigris Institute for Cooperation, and Kent State Koleji. With these projects and grant money from the U.S. Department of State, the Read Center became a catalyst for increased understanding of the Muslim world, became involved in Tract Two diplomacy, and formed new and unusual partnerships. Domestically, with the help of local funders, the Center hosted the first Ohio Global Teachers Institutes, developed study abroad opportunity for area public teachers, and served as a catalyst in developing a global perspective locally. As a leader, I was able to envision a bigger picture.

Leora's Ranch experience during the winter in 1949 taught me to see the big picture and to care for others. Wise leaders who graced the lands of Wyoming early on knew the importance of seeing that big picture. Earlier in the century, Chief Washakie, the Eastern Shoshoni leader, knew that the old days of no-madic life were doomed. He negotiated to obtain good lands for his tribe. Chief Washakie, whose statue is in Washington's Capitol representing Wyo-ming, saw the big picture. Mom and Dad weren't the only ones who knew the importance of caring for others.

How did your childhood experience shape your vision for the future and help you focus on the care of others?

Chapter Two:

Docking Lambs and Shearing Sheep

At the beginning of the 20th Century, Wyoming was home to six million sheep. By the end of World War II, only four million grazed across the state. Like Chief Washakie's nomadic lifestyle was changed by the settlers, the early practices of open range grazing changed Wyoming's lifestyle once again. Conflict with big cattle ranchers caused the number of sheep to dwindle, too. Sheep ranching, unlike raising cattle, requires more manhours. With sheep, extra hands were required for herding, lambing, docking, and shearing

Dad was taking a chance in a business that was in decline. Before the war, Dad had worked for Mom's father, Charlie Schweighart, who ran 2000 head of sheep on his ranch on Cottonwood Creek. Grandpa Charlie had homesteaded in 1915 when wool was needed for uniforms in World War I. Before joining the Army's Calvary in 1942, Dad had seen sheep ranching in its heyday, a growth industry.

But after World War II, protective tariffs were dropped. Labor costs were on the rise. More ranchers were shed lambing instead of having the birthing process take place on the open range. Ranchers with sheds scheduled lambing times earlier in the spring, and therefore, these lambs were heavier at the point of sale in the fall. But the downside was that shed lambing required more hired men. On the other hand, shed lambing reduced the number of dead lambs and ewes due to blizzards like those in 1949.

Either way, ranchers were gambling on the price of lambs, the price of wool, bobcats and coyotes, as well as the weather!

Sheep ranching was on the decline in the 1950s in Wyoming.
Photo credited to Hot Spring County Pioneer Museum and Cultural Center, www.thermpolismuseum.com.

Extra manhours were needed periodically during the spring months—first with lambing, then with docking, and finally with shearing. Within the first weeks of a lamb's birth, a lamb's tail was docked. With the help of Uncle Edgar and hired hands, Mom and Dad did the docking. I sat on the top rail of the fence of the sheep pens and was supposed to be quiet. But from time to time, my curiosity got the better of me, and I pestered them with questions.

"Why are you cutting off their tails?"

Focusing on the work, he was doing, Dad answered simply, "It is better for the lamb."

He didn't go into the real reasons for shorter tails. Docking the tail of the lamb prevented fecal matter from accumulating on the tail and hindquarters. Wool maggot risk was reduced. Blowflies lay eggs on the sheep, and blowflies turn into maggots. These maggots burrow into the flesh and secrete ammonia, poisoning the sheep. Additional flies are then attracted, and the sheep can die within three to six days of the first fly laying eggs.

Then came my next question, "Why are you giving the baby lambs shots? Are they sick?"

Uncle Edgar and the hired hands were inoculating the lambs for a disease called sore mouth. Mom was the first to answer this question, "No, Linda, they are not sick. We are trying to prevent them from being sick."

The next question came quickly as I saw one of the hands cut a part of the lamb's ear off. "Mom, why are they cutting his ear?" I am sure that she heard the concern for the lamb that was in my voice.

Dad answered this time. "We brand them and earmark them so we know they belong to Leora's band of sheep." Branding with black paint was the last task to be done so that the brand was never smeared. Sheep paint was expensive.

Perched on the fence, I watched Mom, Dad and Uncle Edgar dock the week-old lambs. **Family Photo.**

Sheep ranching was labor intensive. Docking, branding with paint, and giving shots all took people to do the work. Plus, the sheep needed to be herded and tended. A sheep herder and a dog or two (in our case Pat Mahoney and his dogs) moved the sheep from one grazing area to another. Dad served as the camp tender—camp tenders brought food and supplies to the sheepherders and assisted in moving the tents or sheep wagon camps from one grazing area to another as dictated by the U.S. Forest Permits and U.S. Bureau of Land Management land use requirements. While we called the place Leora's Ranch, we could have said it was the Government's Ranch. Leora's had less deeded land than land leased from the BLM and the U.S. Forest Service. Leora's Ranch was not unusual in grazing its herd on public land. Most Wyoming ranchers did the same. Even today, 55% of all the land in Wyoming is public land controlled by different agencies of the U.S. government. At Leora's, Pat Mahoney, our Irish herder, was always with our band of sheep—on the U.S. Forest Service mountain land in the summer, at the BLM grazing lands in the fall and spring, and at the ranch's deeded land along the Gooseberry Creek when the band was there for lambing, docking, and shearing.

After the lambing and docking were done, it was time to shear the sheep. In 1949, with Dad taking over after the sudden death of George Hillberry, he had not contracted with a shearing crew early in the season. Therefore, he had to scramble to find sheep shearers who were not already scheduled. So for the spring of 1949, he hired what was called a gypsy crew. They were probably Basques or Roma immigrants. We never really knew. Across the mountain in Buffalo, a lot of Basques from northern Spain were in the sheep business. Roma people from Central Europe were also often called gypsies. Some members of both of these groups hired out as shearers.

Uppy, one of the hired hands, warned me, "These gypsy crews steal little blond-haired, blue-eyed girls."

"Will they steal me? Or was he teasing me?" I looked to Mom worried. She smiled. I think he was teasing me.

Fred asked, "It is true that they bring their families, even children, and live in tents? Dot, will you cook for them?" Mom shook her head, no.

"Darn! We always like all the pies you bake during shearing—coconut cream, apple, pumpkin. Will you still bake for us?" Fred thought more of his belly than the gypsies stealing little girls.

Always thinking ahead, Dad responded, "Let's just hope that they know how to use their shears properly, and can get the shearing done quickly. We don't want any second cuts. We want higher quality wool. After the blizzard, we don't need more troubles."

The conversation around the big kitchen table heightened my interest in the gypsy shearing crew. The gypsy crew arrived and pitched their tents way over by the sheep sheds, across the gulch from the house and barn. Why so far away from the house? Would Mom let me go over there if they had kids to play with? I couldn't even see into their tents to learn if they had children. What a disappointment!

"Mom, can I go see the gypsies? Maybe they have kids…" My voiced trailed off, not knowing if Mom would let me play with gypsy children, even if they had any.

"No, you stay here in the house or by the shearing sheds here by the barn. Stay out of the way. You know Dad won't like it if you are in the way of the men doing their work." Mom was always reminding me how to behave correctly. Or was she a little concerned about the gypsies, too?

But curiosity got the best of me. Gypsies! Here at our ranch! How exotic! Pat Mahoney, our sheep herder, ignited my imagination with stories. I had to figure out how to take a look at the gypsies, and yet I remembered Mom's words to me.

Always a risk taker, I called to Tippy who was always ready to go with me when he wasn't with Dad. "Tippy, you want to go to the corrals and see the shearing?" Mom said it was okay to go to the sheep shearing pens to watch the men working. I figured Tippy would make me feel safe around the gypsies.

Tippy, our faithful border collie, looked up at me, and wagged his tail in agreement. I walked over where Nancy's and my stick horses leaned against the house.

Thinking strategically, I thought, "Hmmm, Nancy is at school. I will ride Nancy's horse."

I giggled to myself. "She won't know."

Her stick horse was faster than mine. At least, Nancy always won races.

Mounted on Nancy's stick horse, I raced Tippy to see the gypsy men at work. Nancy's horse was so fast that we got there in no time!

The sheep shearing pens were like assembly lines where each person performed his particular skill to do a particular job. Climbing up to the highest rail on the fence and trying hard to stay out of the way, I closely observed the smooth operation of herding, capturing the selected ewe, holding the ewe between the shearer's legs, sheering efficiently and safely, and stomping the wool into the big sacks.

The gypsy men bundled in their work clothes looked the same as other hired hands, except they all had the dark shadow of a beard coloring their cheeks. It was kind of a disappointment. I had expected the gypsies to look different, but I didn't know in what way. Learning to be practical from Mom, I forgot about the gypsy men and started to watch the process of shearing.

The wrangler herded a small group of ewes away from the flock. The shearer reached over and grabbed the leg of one, and sat it on its haunches. Gripping the ewe between his knees, he began to cut away the wool, starting at the shoulder. In what seemed like a flash, (actually around three minutes) the fleece fell to the floor. It was important that the shearer cut the fleece in one continuous cut. Because the wool was destined be made into garments for fine ladies or blankets for the Army, the fleeces needed to be long for spinning the wool into thread. Remember Dad said, "No second cuts." Second cuts meant that the fleece was in small sections, and therefore, had less value. Cleanliness of the wool, fineness, length of staple, and strength are all part of the value of the wool.

As I watched, the wrangler tied the fleece into a bundle, and carried the stack of fleeces to the stomping bag. Another man called the tromper gathered up the bundled fleeces, and climbed up to the platform where the long burlap sacks hung. He threw the fleeces in his arms into the sack. The sacks were taller than Dad, or any of the gypsy men.

The shorn ewe was handed off to the next man, who added the special black paint of the Hillberry brand, Z bar Z*, onto the shorn ewe. Sheep paint was expensive. It was a special paint made to last for a year and yet wash out of the wool during the scouring process. Dad didn't want to have any waste. So one of our hired hands painted the brands carefully as the last part of the shearing process. No smears of wet paint on our sheep!

Footnote: George Hillberry had four brands in his name: Z bar Z, ME, bar 71, and CZ according to the Wyoming Livestock Board Brand Unit.

Shearers like these cut the fleeces off in less than 5 minutes! George Hillberry built shearing sheds to help keep the fleeces clean. Lambing and shearing sheds made Leora's Ranch a modern, progressive headquarters.
Photo from Hot Spring County Pioneer Museum and Cultural Center,
www.thermopolismuseum.com

Trompers like this one were a vital part of the
system of sheep shearing at Leora's, too.
Photo from www.wyomingtalesandtrails.com,
photo credited to the Library of Congress.

I moved over close to the platform with the wool sacks. The wool tromper threw the new fleeces into the sack, climbed the ladder, and jumped down into the big tall sack. It surprised me when he began to jump and up and down, packing the wool fleeces tightly. What fun! Imagine having a job just jumping up and down!

After tromping down lots of fleeces, the tromper stepped out of the full sack and onto the platform. He reached over to a shelf and found the largest needle I had ever seen, along with some string, and started to sew up the huge sack. Trompers were full of surprises about them. First, the tromper was a jumping jack, and now he was going to sew? It was a job where you could act like a crazy kid, and then sew like a housewife. Amazing!

I rubbed my nose. Something smelled awful. The greasy lanolin aroma came from the wool fleeces. I decided to move way from all that stink and the greasy looking tromper.

My mind was always jumping like a flea from one thing to another. I started to think about sheep ticks. Did the tromper have sheep ticks on him? Last night at dinner, Pat Mahoney, our sheep herder, warned me that sheep ticks were often found in the wool fleeces. I brushed my coat and Wrangler jeans with my hand to get any sheep ticks off me. I didn't want to die like George Hillberry.

Little did I realize at the time, that watching the shearers at work was a study in systems engineering. Sitting there on the rail, I saw how each special task was necessary in the whole process of shearing as well as docking. If one man failed, the whole system stopped. Dad was under pressure from the aftermath of the blizzard in this first year as the manager of Leora's Ranch. He needed all the ewes shorn properly, with no second cuts or bleeding cuts either. The skills of the sheep shearer affected the value of his wool at market. After a day learning about sheep shearing from the gypsy crew, I was still thinking about it at supper.

That night at supper, I asked, "Dad, you said last night that you would get 45 cents for wool. What does it mean—45 cents for wool?"

"The big sacks are weighed at the sales barn, and each one probably weighs 300 to 500 pounds. I get paid 45 cents per pound of wool. That is around $200 per sack. It takes a lot of sacks to keep this place running," explained Dad always quick with figures.

"Wow, you make lots of money, Dad."

"Barely enough to keep food on this table, Linda," Dad said with a slight smile, waving his hand over the chicken and dumplings. "We just hope that the 45 cents holds. We don't want the wool to sell for less."

Lambing and shearing were special and memorable because these activities brought excitement to our remote ranch life. These events happened only once a year. Like Christmas, I was excited with the hustle and bustle that came with it. Routines, the things that happen on a daily basis, are forgotten. The thought patterns of understanding systems at work were retained in my young brain, in part because this was a once-a -year event of high interest. Leadership training continued—this time in system thinking.

Institutional systems in schools and educational institutions are similar to the shearing process, but less visible. Faculty teach, students apply themselves, parents do their part, custodians clean, the school board members govern, principals lead, secretaries greet, business officials negotiate, the taxpayers pay. Individual expertise is necessary for a quality school. These functions may seem separate, but the institution is truly dependent on each of the other parts. Quality leaders work hard at making sure all aspects of the organization, all components of the system, are aware of and working with all other aspects of the organization.

Perhaps understanding that every aspect of a school was vital for excellence helped the institutions I led receive recognition. Aurora High School received the U.S. Department of Education's National Blue Ribbon, and was recognized by ceremonies in the Rose Garden of the White House for its excellence. The Gerald H. Read Center for International and Intercultural Education at the College of Education, Kent State University was honored with national recognition for excellence in diversity and international education by the National Association of Colleges of Teacher Education for its Outstanding Intercultural Education. These recognitions came to the institutions where I served as the leader—Aurora High School and Kent State's College of Education. In both cases, the institutions were recognized as a whole—all parts were recognized. All systems were working well.

UNDERSTAND SYSTEMS: A LEADERSHIP SKILL

It would be better if everyone worked together as a system,
with the aim for everybody to win.
—Dr. W. Edwards Deming
(a systems thinker with Wyoming roots, too.)

Good leaders are proactive in examining and improving systems—communication with the people served; compliance with accreditation and industry values and expectations; sharing recognition, responsibility, and rewards; and promoting a team approach in achieving the mission of the institution. As with the shearing crew, when all members of the institution do their part with enthusiasm and skill, the mission is accomplished with pride. Rewards come to everyone.

Sheep ranching was always a challenge, with surprises that popped up just when it seemed everything was going smoothly. Spring was here. Winter blizzards were gone. A lot of snow in the mountains meant that there would be plenty of water to irrigate the alfalfa fields and garden in the long hot summer. Soon it would be time to take the sheep to the mountains. That meant trailing them over 35 miles to the leased U.S. Forest mountain lands. For now the sheep were still on the BLM land nearer to the house.

Dad came in from checking on Pat, our sheep herder, and the band with so many new lambs. "Dot, Pat and I found two dead lambs."

A man of few words and always worried about profit and loss, he was probably thinking, "First a blizzard, and now something is killing our lambs. What else could go wrong?" Coyotes were a bother and a worry, but bobcats preying on young lambs were a bigger worry.

"I will have to go hunting." Dad didn't sound like that pleased him.

"Who will you go with you? You mean shoot the bobcats?" queried Mom. She wasn't keen about having the guns brought out.

"No," Dad reassured her, "I mean I need to go hunt where their den is, so I can set a trap." That night he put fresh batteries in big flash lights, took warm coats, hats, and gloves, and set out to find the dens.

The next morning, I was anxious to hear if Dad found the cats. But he hadn't. The worry was evident on his face. Breakfast was not filled with gentle kidding and laughter that morning.

After several nights of no luck, we had a night of really bad luck! Twenty lambs were killed in one night!

Dad complained, "We have ourselves a bobcat killing for the sport. It probably is a queen killing with cubs. She isn't killing for food. This is getting really serious."

This was a crisis bigger than Dad could handle on his own. "Dot, when you go to Vera's on Friday to pick up Nancy, would you ask Edgar to come over Sunday and to bring his horse and gun? He is a really good shot! We need to stop this killer."

Sunday brought rain, always welcomed in this arid land. But why did it come on the night that Dad was going on a bobcat hunt! Uncle Edgar and Aunt Vera drove to the ranch anyway. Dad and Uncle Edgar checked their rifles, and pocketed ammunition. By this time, Dad had figured out that the bobcats were in a special sandstone rock formation between the ranch house and the main highway. He and Uncle Edgar set out in the rain by horseback to kill the varmints!

It was getting late in the evening, and the men had not returned. Aunt Vera and Mom worried that it was getting too late for Nancy. She needed to go to bed. After all, she had school in Grass Creek the next morning. So all of us hopped in our truck and started down the lane to the main highway to take Aunt Vera and Nancy to Grass Creek. One section of our lane was a bit dangerous—the road curved around the hillside, and dropped off to the river bed below. It was scary on a dry day. But now it was slick with rain. The clay-like soil was as slippery as ice when wet. Mom gingerly geared down, drove slowly, and made it with no problems. Once we got to the paved highway, we were safe. No more muddy roads. We drove 20 miles to Aunt Vera's house in the SOHIO camp in Grass Creek.

Mom kissed Nancy goodbye and reminded her, "Nancy, go to bed right away. It is late. We love you."

"Good night," Mom continued.

"Sleep tight, and don't let the bed bugs bite." It was one of Mom's favorite sayings at night. She was having a hard time leaving and going back out in the rain.

Aunt Vera worked at Roy's General Store on Mondays and needed her sleep as well. So Mom and I crawled back in the truck, and headed back to Leora's.

The rain continued as Mom and I started back to the ranch. Paved highways made the travel easy down to the main Highway 120. The soothing smooth ride made it easy for me to fall asleep with my head in Mom's lap. But the paved road quit as we turned off Highway 120 and started down the road to Mullin's and Leora's ranches. Now after a couple of hours of rain, Mom had to gear down as she started forward on the slippery snake of a road. This woke me. I sat up and hung on tight to the handle on the truck door.

Slowly we crept along in the darkness, with rain falling hard on the windshield. The wipers were going very fast, but it was still hard to see. The night was so dark. We came to the part where it was hill, road, and drop-off! But now the rain had made the clay even more slippery—and we were on the side of the road of the big drop off! The truck began to slide. Afraid of going over the edge, Mom stopped the truck. In the blackness of the night, she pulled a scarf over her head and went to see how close the truck's back tires were to the road's edge.

Wet from the hard rain, she quickly got back in the truck. Slowly she backed the truck up, decidiing that if she went faster through the mud, it might be better. Life at Leora's had taught me not to add to Mom's worries. I sat quietly, holding on tight to the door handle.

With careful driving and a little speed, Mom turned the truck around the bend. We were going to make it! I let loose of the door handle . . . a little bit.

When we got to the house, we saw Uncle Edgar's truck and trailer. The men weren't back yet?

Mom and I entered the house, dark and cold. Dad was not there. No one had been there, or they would have started a fire in the stove.

Mom worried, "Those bobcats must be giving Lee and Edgar fits. They're still out hunting." She sighed and continued, "Or stuck in the mud someplace! Let me start a fire, at least."

She mixed the coal and wood to start a quick and warm fire.

"I will stay up for a while and see if they come home, but you need to get to bed. It is way past your bedtime." She said this as she gently rushed me toward the bedroom. I snuggled under the layers of wool blankets, and soon felt the warmth of the fire in the cook stove. Eventually, Mom came to bed, too.

In the morning, Dad and Uncle Edgar still weren't home. She stoked the fire, mixed the pancake batter, and was on her second cup of coffee before the door opened. Two cold and hungry guys entered—muddy overshoes and wet coats were left at the door. Dad and Uncle Edgar leaned their rifles against the water bucket table.

"Did you get the bobcat?" Mom came right to the point.

"Yes, in a trap, but after we spent the night looking for the den. We also shot three cubs. The bobcats won't bother us anymore. No more lambs will be lost to that bobcat or her cubs." Dad answered wearily.

Edgar inquired, "Dot, do you have some hot coffee?"

He looked hungrily over at the pancake batter waiting and the griddle getting hot. "Can't eat breakfast. Too late for work."

He was in such a hurry he couldn't even talk in full sentences.

"No sleep for me now either!" Uncle Edgar stifled a yawn.

Pouring some coffee in a big mug, Mom sent out a warning; "Watch out for the road by the bend by the creek. I nearly slipped off the road into the creek last night. It was scary! Be careful."

Dad looked at her with concern on his face. I walked to where he was sitting. I leaned up close to him, smelling the sweat and rain from the night before.

"I was scared too, but I was brave and hung on tight." I said, not wanting to worry him. He looked so tired.

"Edgar, here, take this cinnamon roll. You better be going before the roads get even worse." Mom urged Edgar out the door. I think she was still concerned over the muddy roads.

Edgar took one last sip of his coffee, and started to put on his coat. "How much damage did that bobcat do?" Edgar knew about the dead lambs and ewes from the blizzard. Now he was concerned for Dad's profit and loss.

"Well, we found 20 that one night, and four on other nights. Overall, in a thousand head of sheep that isn't too bad. But after the blizzard last winter, any loss is too much. Thank you for helping out, Edgar."

"No problem." With a wave of his hand dismissing the thank you, Edgar left to go to work at the SOHIO gas plant at Grass Creek.

Dad was relieved his family was safe; the band of sheep was safe. He wanted to go to bed, but he had animals to feed. Mom brought him steaming pancakes from the grill. I joined him at the table.

Dad had a crisis—the bobcat and the cubs had been eliminated. Dad was a reluctant hunter. Yes, he would kill the deer in the alfalfa field for fresh meat for us to eat. Or when he was in the mountains and needed meat for

28

Pat Mahoney and his dogs, he would kill an elk. But he was not a sport hunter like so many men in Wyoming. Going after bobcats who threatened his livelihood was simply a crisis for him to address. Leadership is about handling a crisis with calm and resolve.

HANDLE CRISIS: A LEADERSHIP MUST

Faced with crisis, the man of character falls back on himself.
He imposes his own stamp of action,
takes responsibility for it, makes it his own.
—Charles de Gaulle

Years later I was leading a U.S. Department of State Partners in Education Project in Kyrgyzstan. This train-the-trainer project centered on developing civic education in this newly independent country. The first part of the project took me to Kyrgyzstan to conduct introductory training, and then a team of seven teachers and ministry officials came to Kent State to develop a civic education curriculum and experience American culture. The last phase of the three-year project was to send experts from Kent State University to work with higher education faculty and elected officials on civic education.

We sent Dr. Vernon Sykes, a faculty member from the political science department who was also a former elected Ohio official, and Dr. William Wilen, a social studies education professor who served as a Fulbright Scholar in other developing countries. While they were attending Washington, D.C. orientations sponsored by American Councils for International Education, word came that demonstrations, riots, and killings had closed down Osh in the southern part of Kyrgyzstan. American Councils cancelled the part of the program where Dr. Wilen was to travel to Osh, and the two professors were told that all was well in the capital, Bishkek. But by the time they arrived in country after the long transcontinental flights, the demonstrators controlled about fifty percent of the country south of Bishkek. Still, the program continued as revised. Bill and Vernon were moved to their home stays in two different parts of Bishkek. They were assured that that capital city was safe.

This proved to be wrong. Demonstrations broke out in the city center the next morning. As you can imagine, all were concerned for the professors' safety. Bill went to an internet café near his home-stay apartment and connected with American Councils, his family, and us at Kent State University. A plan developed to move them closer to the American Embassy for safety's sake. So the next day they packed up their things, and moved to the Pinara Hotel near an area where U.S. Marines were housed. This was within sight of the Parliament Building. We all thought this was the safest place in the country.

But we learned that wasn't necessarily the case. Demonstrating crowds grew, and the city center was looted. No one seemed to be in charge; there was no law and order. The main international airport was rumored to be closed. Accurate and timely information was hard to get. Some of the demonstrators wore pink ribbons, and soon the television crews were calling this the Pink or Tulip Revolution. Then to our dismay, the Parliament Building was over taken by the demonstrators. Our concern for Bill and Vernon's safety increased.

We were fortunate that in the same touristic-oriented hotel where I had stayed during the first phase of this grant, Bill and Vernon had access to the internet. With emails, they were able to stay in touch with us at Kent State University, their families, and the American Councils in Washington, D.C., as well as the Embassy officials in Bishket. With other American and international guests now crowded in the Pinara Hotel, they barricaded the doors, and stayed away from the windows.

After a few days of great concern, things began to quiet. A new government was installed. Order returned; the airport opened. But it was not the ideal time to teach about civic engagement with university professors or citizens. The program was cancelled. With the help of the American Embassy, the two professors evacuated via Istanbul to Washington, D.C. The crisis was over. In fact, Dr. Wilen published an article to share his experience of being in the middle of the Pink Revolution. His article helped other social studies educators learn about surviving a revolution.

Certainly in planning the program for the three-year grant, we did not anticipate a revolution. Kent State was not heavily involved in development projects globally in those years. There was no risk management team on campus to help bring the two professors home safely. Like Dad dealing with the killer bobcat, I found myself handling a crisis without having experience. Bobcats and coyotes roamed the range all of the time. Dad knew this. Yet, the killing of 20 lambs in one night created a crisis to deal with swiftly. In this grant-funded project, we were used to changing activities and adapting goals as we advanced the work. But none of us had expected a coup of the country's government. Both Dad and I relied on others with more experience (Uncle Edgar and American Embassy/American Councils) to help solve our crises. With experience, leadership becomes easier. Problems were opportunities to be solved—without fuss.

Dad took over the lease of Leora's Ranch without ever having been a top manager. In the spring of 1949 Dad got $1 a pound for wool, much more than the 45 cents expected. The downward trend of wool prices after World War II were offset by the rising prices of wool after the Blizzard of 1949. This was like hitting the jack pot! The sheep business might be in decline, but with prices like this more people would be wanting to raise sheep. This was a hopeful sign for Dad and our family.

Events at the ranch were often unpredictable. Yet at the same time, nothing seemed impossible. Leadership is about designing systems that work, but also about handling crisis when they come. Another Wyoming native and expert in systems thinking, Dr. W. Edwards Deming, reminds us about the importance of leaders undertanding systems, "*It would be better if everyone worked together as a system, with the aim for everybody to win.*"

Even the best systems have to deal with the unexpected. Charles de Gaulle reminds us, "*Faced with crisis, the man of character falls back on himself. He imposes his own stamp of action, takes responsibility for it, makes it his own.*" In what way did your early life experiences teach you about how to plan proactively and to handle the unexpected?

Chapter Three:

Pat Mahoney and the Sheep Wagon

One of the personal benefits of each lambing and shearing season was that Pat Mahoney, the sheep herder, and his sheep wagon moved off the Bureau of Land Management (BLM) land, and snuggled into a corner by the bunk house.

Oh, the sheep wagon— in my young eyes, it was a magical home. Its design efficiency and simplicity fascinated me. Cupboards, stove, and bed were designed to maximize space—in fact, the sheep wagon was inspiration for Wally Byam and his Airstream campers. The stove was just inside the door, and was a smaller version of Mom's cast iron kitchen stove. Cupboards were built over the stove and held spices and non-perishables for us to explore. Shelves over the cushioned benches and the bed held books—usually lots of Zane Grey westerns well-worn from frequent readings. The bed was in the back of the wagon, placed high above the storage space. A flip-up table magically appeared in the middle. Built-in benches along the sides had storage underneath and cushions on top. They were the seats for the pop-up table.

Sheep wagons, high enough to be moved over rough Wyoming terrain, were first designed and made by a Rawlins, Wyoming, blacksmith, James Candlish in 1884. By 1904 sheep wagons were being built locally by D.V. Bayne of nearby Thermopolis. The practical design that could be moved by mule, a team of horses, or a truck fascinated me as a child, and still delights me.

Pat's sheep wagon was a story teller's stage and a playhouse
for imaginations to create a new world for the day or perhaps the future.
The sheep wagon at the Museum of the Rockies,
Bozeman, Montana, still fascinates me today.
Family photo.

A friend of George Hillberry, Pat Mahoney was all Irish. George's heritage was Scottish. He immigrated from the Isle of Man. The similar cultures of their Irish and Scottish homelands had made the two men friends. Pat worked for George for three years. Loyal to the Hillberry family after the death of George, Pat stayed on to work for Dad. Dad said that Pat was straight out of the Steinbeck book, *Grapes of Wrath.* He had picked cotton and watermelons as he moved across the continent finding work. His path led him to George Hillberry and the job on this ranch. Most of the other sheep ranchers hired

Basques from Spain. The Basques came from high in the Pyrenees, Northern Spain, and came under contract with the Western Range Association beginning in 1940s due to the severe labor shortage during World War II.

Fortunately for me, not all the days and nights brought snow or rain storms. Some evenings when lambing or shearing was going on and his sheep were in the sheds at the ranch headquarters, Pat would invite me to come out to the sheep wagon for stories. Grandma Schweighart had given us a silver—not red—toy wagon last Christmas. I laid a bed of soft wool quilts in my toy wagon, and pulled it over to Pat's sheep wagon. Snuggled deep in the bedding's warm comfort, I was ready for my evening treat. Pat would come out and sit in the doorway of the wagon with his feet balanced on the tongue. Tippy, usually close to me, joined us as a silent companion. And the stories would start.

As I listened, I was in imagination heaven. Listening to his thick Irish brogue, I was enthralled. I was transposed from Wyoming's arid landscape to the green hills of Ireland, from the 1940s to times gone by. I was spellbound by the mystery of the stories woven to keep the listener engaged to the very end. I didn't have many books. We had no television. But I did have an Irish storyteller to ignite my imagination.

We subscribed to the *Worland Daily News*, delivered twice a week with the mail. *Newsweek* and *Saturday Evening Post* arrived with eager anticipation weekly. We listened to KWOR radio for news and music, but I don't remember listening to stories on the radio in those years. The local AM radio station wasn't on the air for too many hours, and other radio stations were too far away for their signals to come to this remote location surrounded by hills. Pat's stories were treats to be savored like the first strawberries of spring.

In this stark, sagebrush steppe land where antelope, mule deer, sage grouse, and coyotes were plentiful, Pat Mahoney brought fairies, pookas, mermaids, leprechauns, as well as the good luck of butterflies. I was introduced to Macha, the Goddess of the Horses, and could almost hear the melodies of the harp. In contrast to our harsh surroundings, Pat brought a land of fantasy. Of all the memories in my life, Pat Mahoney and his stories are some of my fondest. Little did I know that my later work would introduce me to a real Irish storyteller, or *sheanchai*, Batt Burns. Nor did I know that I would spend two decades traveling around the world and hosting scores of students, teachers, and scholars from many different countries, legends, and cultures. My appetite was enhanced by these stories of the "old country" shared by Pat Mahoney.

My prized possession for years was a Hop-A-Long Cassidy Pocket Knife given to me by Pat Mahoney. He said it was for cutting off sheep ticks.
Photo: Auction Exchange USA. https://www.mylocal auction.com. Retrieved July 21, 2021.

It was the custom for the sheepherders to go to Worland or Thermopolis for a get-a-way before moving to the high country for the summer. The summer range was even more isolated from people and conveniences than the ranch. After lambing was done, Dad took Pat to Worland and picked him up several days later. When Pat came back to the ranch, he brought me a Hop-A-Long Cassidy pocket knife. He said it was to cut off the sheep ticks. I am sure he was still missing his friend George Hillberry, who had four boys. Having a little girl around the ranch brought a bit of novelty to his rural life. Even though a pocket knife was a rather unusual gift for a young girl, I was allowed to keep it. It was a prized possession for many years.

STORY TELLING: A LEADERSHIP TOOL

Stories constitute the single most
powerful weapon in a leader's arsenal.
— Dr. Howard Gardner, Harvard University.

My appreciation of the art of storytelling helped me throughout my leadership experience.

Later when I was the director at Kent State University, the university was awarded a grant from the U.S. Embassy in Ankara, Turkey. In conjunction with Turkey's Ataturk Dam regional development project, this project's focus was to provide support for the Kurdish and Turkish women in this rapidly changing area. Irrigation was now available to these former dry land farmers. Winter wheat was abandoned, and now corn and cotton were growing, and electricity became available in remote villages. The Southeastern Anatolia Project (GAP in Turkish) was modeled after the Tennessee Valley Authority.

Our project was another train-the-trainer program using storytelling as the key method of communication since most the women that Turkish government wanted to reach were illiterate. Oral storytelling traditions were rich in the Kurdish and Turkish cultures. We modelled their cultural tradition, and used stories to develop civic engagement, to improve maternal health, and to highlight ways young women could contribute to families economically.

This development project started with several conferences for key stakeholders in southeastern Turkey. Sanli Urfa and Mardin, both ancient cities, were the sites for these conferences. At these trainings, we identified natural women leaders and male allies, and invited twenty of them to Kent State University for additional training, immersion in American life, and the opportunity to net-work with each other. These women and men then returned to Mardin and Sanli Urfa and sponsored regional trainings for more local women. The cap-stone of the project was to be a large international training conference with Syrian, Iranian, and Iraqi women leaders–all countries sharing the same waters of the Tigris and Euphrates Rivers now dammed by the Ataturk Dam project.

One of the goals of the project was to teach these often-isolated women to learn how to access governmental and non-governmental agencies for help. So when the groups came to Kent State University, we connected these Turkish women and men with local and Ohio governmental officials as well as local women leaders who had success interacting with regional governmental agencies. Instead of the traditional PowerPoint presentation about their work, current laws, or such, we simply had all of these elected or activist leaders tell their personal stories. These stories were impactful. The first woman Ohio Secretary of State, Jennifer Brunner, brought tears to the whole audience as she told her story of determination, sacrifice, and success. Rita, a local woman had fought the city hall resistance in creating a day care, persisted, and finally came to compromises that pleased both the conservative zoning board and the young entrepreneur. Stories are powerful, memorable, and often inspired our young Turkish visitors to action.

Part of the leadership training was to help the local Turkish women also develop skills that added income to their families. Coming from a conservative Muslim area where women were often kept at home, the Turkish government still wanted these women to be able to have some independence economically. So participants also heard the stories told by local Ohio women entrepreneurs with cottage businesses. We heard stories of how hobbies often become in-come producing businesses. Tatting hand-made lace, pickling beets and peppers, making lavender soaps and candles were now for-profit businesses. No brochures were given; no PowerPoints were used. We simply asked our presenters to tell their stories. All of this was done with simultaneous trans-lation (English to Turkish). Can you imagine how hard it would have been if data, charts, quotes, and key points were used in all the presentations? All translations are difficult. Stories are easier to translate than data and scientific language, and our participants remembered the stories easily.

When the Turkish guests returned home to plan second training confer-ences in Sanli Urfa and Mardin, these newly inspired trainers once again used the same storytelling methods. Their presenters also told their stories in the local languages—Kurdish or Turkish—targeting the rural women in small vil-lages being transformed by electricity and scientific farming. This was an area of rapid and abrupt change, which brought water to dry-land farming region. This was documented not only by scientific data, but by individual stories of change. The Turkish government wisely documented this change through photographs to assist the illiterate citizens to see and accept the change that they were living.

On a rainy night, not unlike the rainy night of the bobcat hunt, the trainer team of Americans and Turkish hosts were guests at a local farmer's home in a small village. The tenant farmer said, with the help of our translator, "As a young man I went to help build the dam. I thought that I would never see the results. And now in just a few years, I am entertaining international guests in my home, own a tractor and television set, and hope to send my daughters to college."

We enjoyed his prosperity and hospitality while sitting on cushions dec-orating the perimeter of the room. A banquet of homecooked food was spread on the tablecloth on the floor in front of us. The fresh lamb chops and hot peppers were delicious. I am sure that his family has heard the story of the night he entertained these American visitors many times. Stories are remem-bered and passed along to generations.

Pat Mahoney's storytelling affected me early on; storytelling served me well as the director of this large development grant decades later. Storytelling would help Turkish women leap into the 21st Century economically, in terms of civic engagement, and in terms of the personal belief that they could shape their own futures.

The sheep wagon was more than a storytelling theatre. In the summer the band of sheep went to the mountains, and the steep mountain terrain made it impossible for the sheep wagon to serve as Pat's house. So in the summer, he camped in a tent that was moved frequently to keep him and the sheep near fresh grass. For Nancy and I, the fact that the sheep wagon was left parked near the bunk house was a wonderful childhood benefit.

Pat Mahony's sheep wagon became an imagination center—a playhouse where Nancy (home from school) and I could make mud pies in our toy dishes, sprinkle the pies with chili powder left behind in the cupboards! Our dolls were our characters as we created our own imaginative stories of faraway places. Our stick horses were broncs to be ridden, and we pretended to be Deb Copenhaven and Jim Soldiers. We knew about these all-star professional cowboys from small comic-style booklets that came with our Wrangler jeans. Generations later, many heroes like Superman came from comic books. But our comic booklets featured the stars of the Professional Rodeo Cowboy Association with help from the marketing team at the new (started in 1947) denim jean company, Wrangler.

WRANGLER JEANS HEROS *Small comic-style booklets showcased great moments in Jim Shoulders All Around Cowboy Days. The rodeo stars were our childhood heroes.*
Photo: **https://www.mycomicshop.com/search?TID=541331**

Nancy and I created our own narratives, in what we might now call dramatic play. We called it "pretend." On any given day, Nancy was a teacher and I was her student. The next day, we were ranchers moving cattle to the mountains, and the sheep wagon was the chuck wagon serving up hot beans and biscuits to hungry cowhands. Sometimes she was the mother, and I was the child. Dolls were put to bed and covered with the quilts left behind.

Children pretend and use their imaginations to bring meaning to the world around them. Pat Mahoney's stories fueled our imagination and dramatic play resulted. The sheep wagon made this memorable to us, part of my early experience.

And like the storytelling above, this imaginative play would serve me as a director of an international center at Kent State University years later. For thirteen years, Kent State University was awarded the International Leaders in Education Program (ILEP), sponsored by the U.S. Department of State. This program brought secondary teachers from around the world to Kent State University for a semester of academic work, internships in the public schools, and immersion in American and each other's cultures.

One of the ways these global teachers shared their culture with others was through informal *Cultural Dialogues*. Universities often have lectures on campus—cultural dialogues were different. The design of the cultural dialogues was influenced by immersion into a "pretend" experience, much like Nancy and I were doing in Pat Mahoney's sheep wagon.

We asked the global teachers to create a scenario that would put the audience in a special moment, in a special place—to experience their culture, not just learn facts about their country. Since one of the goals of the ILEP program was to gain respect and understanding of cross-cultural work, we assigned diverse teams of teachers from different countries to design these experiences around a common theme such as *the movement of people around the world* or *the day in a life of a woman*, or *weddings, funerals, and unknown holidays.*

The *Cultural Dialogues* were not a show-and-tell; they were not histories nor travelogues. Instead these global teachers had to create an experiential learning opportunity for the audience. The hour-long performance was a form of applied improvisation. Developing an appreciation of other cultures is advanced through *emotions* as well as gaining *knowledge.* Our *Cultural Dialogues* did just that. This pretend immersion experience became widely popular with the teachers planning them as well as the attendees—students, faculty, and even community members.

IMPROVISATION: A LEADERSHIP TOOL

We don't stop playing because we grow old;
we grow old because we stop playing.
—George Bernard Shaw

Paired groups had to really examine their own culture and to think deeply about connections with the other assigned country. The skills of *leaping in* and *letting go* were evident as teams had difficulty understanding other cultural norms when accomplishing the assigned tasks. Often the script was developed moments before (or even during) the program. Two contrasting cultures (Indonesians and Senegalese, for example) had to agree on how to develop an hour-long program. Risk taking? You bet. And yet, the audience loved these presentations, because they were playful, real and touched the heart. The community members, students, and faculty in attendance felt they experienced a moment in another culture. The audience had to "pretend", too. They were touched both cognitively and emotionally.

One year we used the theme of the movement of people around the world. The scholars had to demonstrate something about the movement of people and how it affected their culture, their history. Moroccans and Ghanaians teachers roleplayed slave traders taking a slave to market in Ghana. The "Ghanaian slave," in chains and half crawling through the seated audience, was being led by a large Moroccan man.

The enslaved man was crying, "Africa, oh Africa, where are you??? Save me!!! Save me, Africa!!"

No one in the audience, including me, had ever thought about African involvement in the slave trade. Why didn't African nations resist the slave traders and try to save their own? This began to haunt me and caused me to consider the role of Africans in the American slave trade. Why didn't they fight against the selling of their brothers and sisters? It inspired me to research the slave trade more deeply, from an African point of view—something that was not covered in my American history books. His cry of "Africa, Oh Africa, where are you?" was a shock that I will never forget. The role playing was powerful.

Cultural Dialogues were designed to teach in a unique way, and yet were grounded in the freedom that Nancy and I had to pretend daily in the sheep wagon. While we didn't have a real fire in the sheep wagon's stove to bake our mud pies, we used solar energy to bake them. Wyoming's hot sun, even in late spring, burned! Mom made us wear new red felt hats when we were outside. We didn't have sunscreen. Just like Dad, we grabbed our hats as we ran out the door to play. We thought we were pretty fancy in these hats and were proud to replace our old straw hats with the red felt ones.

Taking a break from playing in the sheep wagon, we also enjoyed riding our bikes. Because the dirt roads were often rutted with dried mud, we had to be careful riding up and down the lane to the house. The bikes were pretty special to us. Mom knew that and would use that later as a bribe!

Nancy and I pose on our bikes, wearing our new red felt cowboy hats, too. Notice the sheep wagon in the background. ***Family Photo***

Mom wanted me to stop sucking my thumb. She tried everything. In desperation, she painted my nails with something that tasted hot whenever I started to suck. It didn't stop me. I still sucked my thumb. I let the tears flow freely until the burn of the hot pepper waned. I suffered through it—I was still a thumb sucker.

Then she decided to raise the stakes really high. She threatened to take away my new tricycle. She knew how proud I was of it. But I was stubborn.

I simply said, "I have other things to play with. I was okay before I had it. I don't need it."

If I had my thumb and the silky ribbon edging on a blanket for my fingers to stroke, I could go to sleep anywhere. In fact, that summer, I did! I fell asleep one evening standing up, sucking my thumb, wedged between the night stand and the bed, with my fingers running up and down the edging on the bed's blanket.

Our hired hand, Fred Shyrack, teased me about it all summer. I was glad when haying was over, and he wasn't around anymore. But years later at the Worland Farm Auction, we saw each other. I was visiting Dad and Mom and had gone to the weekly auction with Dad.

Dad reintroduced us. "Fred, you remember our youngest daughter, Linda."

Fred smiled, and said without missing a beat, "Lee, is this the one who went to sleep standing up, sucking her thumb?"

Sometimes, you are known for your bad habits even years later—another leadership lesson from Leora's. Mom finally gave up her fight with me over thumb sucking. After I started school, I finally quit sucking my thumb. But for years I continued to rub the silk ribbon on the blankets when I needed comforting.

Mom learned from her mistakes—nothing she tried worked. I had outlasted her. She found herself in a hole and quit digging.

LEARN FROM MISTAKES: A LEADERSHIP MUST

When you find yourself in a hole, quit digging.
—Will Rogers

Later I was the one who had to learn to "stop digging holes." As a new principal in Aurora City Schools, I was eager to bring innovation and pride to the elementary building that housed all kindergartners and fifth graders of the district as well as a neighborhood school for grades 1-4. The school was really the old high school, which had been connected to an old elementary building. The building was poorly maintained, and the teachers had been on strike for a month the previous year. Morale was low.

Always an optimist, I wanted to build a new culture of pride. At a faculty meeting, I announced that a Golden Trash Can Award would be presented weekly to the classroom that maintained the highest level of cleanliness and care. I proudly displayed the bright golden trash cans for each hallway. I had invited the custodians to the faculty meeting and recruited them to help me judge the new competition. They were pleased to be part of the new initiative. As I announced the competition, I noticed that the teachers nodded in agreement.

But on Friday of the first week, can you imagine how shocked I was when I learned that several of the fifth-grade teachers had trashed the room of a co-worker while he was at lunch? Steve always had a neat and tidy room. Ron and the others knew Steve would always win the fifth-grade hall's Golden Trash Can Award. So they were preventing it by trashing his room!

I had failed to see this whole competition from the teacher's point of view. I had read the nods as agreement. That was a big mistake. I learned the hard way that the best idea (even if this may not have been the best idea) can go astray without involving others in the decision making.

Needless to stay, we did not continue the Golden Trash Can competition. But we did have a continued conversation about everyone's responsibility to maintain the cleanliness of the school. I let the mischievous fifth-grade teachers go without any reprimand—it was my mistake that led them astray. Ron, the instigator of the trashing, and Steve stayed friends for life, and they would tell this story in informal gatherings with lots of laughter.

Just like Mom learned that I was going to resist every method she tried to get me to stop sucking my thumb, I quickly abandoned the idea of a trash can award. Turning mistakes into learning opportunities helps the leader earn respect, strengthens the morale of the team, provides an opportunity to lead by example, and builds trust. Mom led by example. I had to fail on my own before really learning. But I kept one of those golden trash cans under my desk the whole time I served as a principal in a school as a reminder of the need to learn from past mistakes.

I never went to kindergarten. I did not attend pre-school or play groups. Mom and Dad didn't have much time for Nancy and me. They were busy with gardens to harvest, fields of alfalfa to irrigate, sheep to move to new pastures, and hauling water for daily use. Yet, our imaginative play in the sheep wagon enabled us to develop self-reliance, creative problem solving, and independence—all important leadership characteristics.

Dr. Howard Gardner, a professor at Harvard University, makes the case for storytelling as a leadership tool, explaining that *Stories constitute the single most powerful weapon in a leader's arsenal.* Pat Mahoney gave me the gift of storytelling for my leadership arsenal.

The late writer George Bernard Shaw also reminds us that improvisation, or "pretend" as we called it, is a life skill in many different situations. Shaw says, *"We don't stop playing because we grow old, we grow old because we stop playing."* Set some parameters to the improvisation, and it becomes a powerful tool for problem solving and imagining the future.

We can live in a pretend world part of the time, but leaders also need to be grounded. We also need to know when to quit. Our resident philosopher, Will Rogers, said it simply: *"When you find yourself in a hole, quit digging."* Mom gave up. But she did so without damaging our relationship or making me feel bad about sucking my thumb. Quitting at the right time with the right tone is a vital characteristic of leaders.

How did your play patterns affect your life? Your leadership abilities? And do you ever wonder why we stop pretending?

Chapter Four:

Branding Calves and Raising Bulls

June kicked off a season of fun activities. Pat Mahoney and Dad trailed the sheep 35 miles to the mountain range for the summer. Schools were out; Nancy was home from Aunt Vera's. It was time now for branding. Area ranchers depended on each other when branding cattle. Brandings also were social gatherings for lonely housewives. In the winter months, square dances were held at the local schools, and neighbors hosted card parties where pinochle was the favorite game. But in the early summer, ranchers up and down the creek scheduled their brandings so they could help each other. It was a month that involved going from branding to branding. Volunteer help made the process of branding a big social activity for us all.

The old adage, "you scratch my back, and I will scratch yours," inspired the network of neighboring ranchers who were recruited as free help. It took many able men to brand a herd of cattle. First the cow and calves were rounded up from the BLM grazing lands, and brought to the ranch. With the cows and calves corralled, the branding began. Mounted on a horse, the roper selected a calf to be branded and roped it. Next, he led the calf over to the branding fire and the waiting red-hot branding irons. Wranglers, usually younger more able ranch hands, threw the calf to the ground and held it down. Another neighbor seared the V open A V brand on our calves. Bulls were castrated, while another rancher inoculated and earmarked all of the calves. Notice that an observable system was alive and well here, too. I stood on the rails of the corral and observed the system working firsthand.

The reputation of the ranch was also based on our roast beef, baked beans, pies, and freshly baked bread. Mom and Dad prided themselves that the food at Leora's Ranch brandings was excellent and plentiful. This helped to convince busy ranchers and hands to help. Now it was our turn to begiin the branding. Mom was busy getting ready.

As she prepared the grocery list, I inquired in the winey voice kids use when they want something. "Mom, can we have orange pop? Root beer? Please, pretty pleeeeease."

We never had soda pop to drink. Pop only appeared at brandings. And I was pleased when we went to Worland to buy all the groceries for the big gathering that pop was in the bag.

On the day of the branding, makeshift tables were made from saw horses and wooden planks. Blankets were spread for picnicking crews. Kitchen chairs for gossipy women created corrals for toddlers. Older children ran around playing tag and sneaking cookies.

Dad knew exactly who to invite to get the branding done effectively. He avoided those who brought their own beer and who only thought about socializing. He knew he needed young hands to wrangle the calves. Dad was an excellent roper, and often served in that capacity at other ranches, but he needed to be in charge here. Another good roper was needed in the corral. Who was going to be the inoculator? Who knew how to castrate without too much bleeding? Inviting area ranchers was strategic, and it had to be done with some thought.

Branding day started early. I snuggled in my bed, nestled next to Nancy in the morning chill. But I could hear Mom in the kitchen starting the baking and cooking. Dad was giving directions to the hired hands about the round up. Even though it was before sunrise, Nancy and I leaped from bed. We did not want to miss anything. The men ate quickly, and then left.

As we helped in the kitchen, I queried Mom: "Why do they brand the little calves with a hot iron? Doesn't it hurt?"

Mom, busy with rolling pie crust, sighed. "Branding is part of cattle ranching. We give each of the new calves a brand so everyone knows they belong to us. It is like our name—Brunk. The brand says the calf belongs to our family. Our brand is V open A, V. The open A is like this." She shows us with her two fingers: "V (hand held up). Open A (hand inverted). V (hand held up)."

"Like this?" we mimicked, moving our hands in the V open A V way playfully.

The cattle, unlike the sheep who were owned by Leora, belonged to Dad and Mom. It was pretty neat that they had the V open A V brand on them! They were ours.

Mom continued, a natural teacher, even though she only had an eighth-grade education in a one-room school house usually attended by only her brothers and sisters: "We also give them shots so they don't get sick. Just like Dr. Vicklund gives you shots to make you healthy."

Still full of questions, I asked, "What do they do to the bull calves?"

The ever practical parent, Mom replied, "It is called castration. Bulls become steers. Steers are worth more than bulls when they are sold for beef."

She did not go on to explain that castrating helped ease the handling of cattle in feeding pens on their way to market. Steers also gained weight differently, with increased marbling and tenderness of the beefsteak. Both she and Dad were always thinking of the profit and loss.

We could hear the bawling of the cows and calves corralled down the hill as we went outside. Dust on the road leading to the ranch announced the arriving neighbors as well. The smell of the campfire let us know that the branding irons were getting hot.

Ropers quickly select the calf for branding, and wranglers wrestle the calf to the ground. **Family photo.**

At Leora's, calves were branded with Dad's V Open A V brand. Nancy and I still own this brand. **Family Photo.**

As the actual branding began, I left the crowd of kids laughing and talking. I called to Tippy. Together Tippy and I ran over to the corrals to watch the men working. Nate Brown from Grass Creek was on his horse roping. Didn't Nate also rope in the rodeos? Wasn't that Knute Carlson—Dad had worked for him—with the branding iron? Two younger men I didn't know were on the ground holding the outstretched calf. And then came Bill Mullins, our neighbor to the west, holding the tools for cutting the bulls. Johnny Rankin, married to our cousin Elaine, looked like he was imitating Dr. Vicklund by inserting the needle into the medicine bottle.

Dad had assembled men with expertise to help him with the many processes of the branding day. These were men he knew well, and they did their assigned role reliably. Building networks is a tool necessary for any leader.

BUILD NETWORKS: A LEADERSHIP MUST

A man only learns in two ways—one by reading,
and the other by association with smarter people.
–Will Rogers

Knowing the expertise needed was key to a successful branding. Building a network of experts was exactly what I did as a director at Kent State University. I needed connections for new projects locally and across the world, as well as to improve the image of the international center in the campus community. So in my capacity as director, I developed a Professional Advisory Council for the Gerald H. Read Center for International and Intercultural Education. Like Dad asking selected neighbors and friends, I identified some key organizations and made calls recruiting representatives to form this panel of experts. In a short time my recruitment efforts paid off. Members of the United States Olympic Committee, World Bank, International Baccalaureate World Schools, the Consortium for Overseas Student Teaching, the Comparative and International Education Society, Ontario's Ministry of Education, The College of The Bahamas, Chapters India, and more were all serving the Gerald H. Read Center for International and Intercultural Education.

Although these 11 people came to campus only once or twice a year at their own expense (just like the neighbors at the branding), we learned from the Advisory Board's perceptions, connections, and expertise. For example, Kent State University's Early Childhood Program was the first in the world to have all graduates eligible for the International Baccalaureate World Schools teacher's certificate. Kent State became the graduate school of education for the College of The Bahamas, educating many of the country's principals and guidance counselors.

The Advisory Board's presence on campus provided an audience of experts to showcase our own Kent State faculty's global innovations and research. This was a motivator for our faculty to take risks globally. Our Board traveled to New York; Washington, D.C.; Florence, Italy; and Nassau, Bahamas and sponsored collaborative initiatives expanding Kent State's influence and impact. Today the board is a legacy that remains part of the Gerald H. Read Center for International and Intercultural Education.

Like the branding at Leora's, the Professional Advisory Board meetings always included a social dimension to celebrate with top university administration, faculty, and local partners. Combining the outside expertise with the social aspects heightened pride in the international work we were doing. I learned from Mom and Dad that having good food, a festive setting, a well-planned and executed event accomplished even bigger goals.

In an interview with my 96-year-old Uncle Carl (a Wyoming Cowboy Hall of Fame recipient) for the purpose of this book, he said that brandings today don't involve the same sense of community. Many ranchers do the branding by themselves using technologies to earmark, brand, castrate, and inoculate. Uncle Carl said that the sense of community is lost without the depending on each other to accomplish the task. Outside networks validate the successes of the organization, and increase awareness of the quality of work done within the organization. Leadership can be lonely—these networks often provide social confirmation for leaders in making day-to-day decisions.

At Leora's, branding was a social activity as well as a function of necessity for cattle ranchers. When the work was all done, the assembled crew drank cold Coors beer and ate Rocky Mountain oysters. Rocky Mountain oysters are bull calf testicles, skinned, coated with flour, pepper and salt, and then deep fried. This delicacy was served to the men in return for the hard work of the day. Mom's big cast-iron skillets sizzled on the old kitchen stove. Beers were popped open and consumed in long pulls.

The sun was getting lower over the mountains in the west, and the branding fires were extinguished. No more dishes needed to be washed, and cows and calves were chewing their cuds. Dust on the road now was an indication that the branding day was over, and people were leaving. Exhausted from the hard work, the excitement, and the long day, we all happily gathered in the house and shared stories learned from the neighbors. Branding at Leora's was a necessary task for cattle ranchers like Dad, but a great social event for Mom, Nancy, and me, too. Branding was done until next spring. Who would be the next one coming down the road and making dust?

In a few days, we did have visitors from afar. Aunt Sadie and Aunt Dora, relatives of Mom's father, Charlie Schweighart, came to see us all the way from Sandusky, Ohio.

Aunt Dora and, Aunt Sadie, posing here with Grandma Schweighart and a friend, brought us scratchy wool swimming suits. They lived on Lake Erie in Ohio. Water is not scarce there like it was at Leora's. **Family Photo**

After greetings and introductions were exchanged, Aunt Sadie handed Nancy and me packages. She watched with anticipation as we tore them open. Boy, was I disappointed! Bathing suits in pink and yellow? No toys!

We didn't have anywhere to go swimming—Leora's was a remote ranch on Gooseberry Creek that often didn't have much water. Even the well water on the ranch was not fit for us to drink. We had to haul water from a neighbor's well or bring it from Grass Creek for drinking, cooking, and bathing. When Gooseberry Creek had enough water, we did go there in the summer, but not to swim. We took our baths there. And we didn't wear clothes to take a bath! What a silly gift, I thought.

Reluctantly, I tried it on. . . that only made things worse! The suit was made from scratchy wool. I hated how it felt on my skin. Ugh, it was hard to be polite, but a look from Mom told me I had better try.

Maybe sensing that the gifts were not well received, Aunt Sadie decided to go in a different direction. She asked, "What do you want to be when you grow up?" She probably asked that of all her grandchildren.

I stood tall—at least for me, as I was always the shortest for my age. I knew this answer for sure. I was proud of my thoughts for the future. I often told others what I wanted to be when I grew up.

"I want to be a rancher, who runs only bulls, and marries an Indian."

The shock on her face took me back. Why did she look as though this wasn't a good answer? I was definite about this career path.

Now looking back at this exchange, I am sure that Aunt Sadie was wondering why I wanted to be a rancher and not a rancher's wife? Why did I want to run only bulls? Didn't the ranches sell calves that brought the cash to run the ranch? If you only had bulls, how could you have calves? Why would anyone want to marry an Indian? I am sure she thought that this little girl needs a lot of help and guidance!

And yet, you know enough of my story by now to know that the ranch was my life. I was confirming even then that I wanted a leadership position. I wanted to run the ranch, not stay at the house and cook for the crew. I was modeling my hopes and dreams after Dad, not Mom.

Yet, I did not know any women ranchers—didn't Leora have to hire someone to run her ranch when her husband died? I don't have many memories of watching Mom bake and cook, wash clothes, plant the garden, haul water, clean the house. Those tasks happened daily, were routine, and therefore weren't that memorable. Lambing, shearing, and branding were big events, with lots of people, excitement, and new routines. They were memorable. Was that the attraction of being a rancher, as opposed to a rancher's wife?

It didn't occur to me that a woman could *not* be a boss. It didn't enter my head. Today, one in eleven Wyoming ranches are headed by a woman. Was I seeing into the future at what was *possible* and *likely?* I prepared to be a teacher, but only taught for three early years. The rest of my career, I served as an educational leader. I was aiming for leadership roles the summer I turned four.

Aunt Sadie continued to question me, "Why do you want to run a bulls-only ranch? Does that happen?" She looked at Mom for the answer to the last question.

Looking back on this now, I wonder where I did get this notion? Had there been a table discussion about the use of artificial insemination making bulls-only ranches financially viable by selling semen? Artificial insemination was not used in those years in raising beef cattle in Wyoming. In fact, according to my interview with Cousin Earnie Beckley in preparation for this book, artificial insemination wasn't used in the area until decades later. But it was Bobby Brunk, my cousin and summertime helper for Dad, who much later was the first rancher to use artificial insemination at his Nowood River ranch near Tensleep. Was I, like Cousin Bobby, ahead of my time, or didn't I understand cattle ranching?

A future orientation is vital for good leadership. This is true particularly in schools that are educating students for the future. As a school principal and university administrator, I continually read all about future trends, attended workshops and conferences to keep abreast of technologies and research innovations for education, learning theories, and management. Early on, I seemed to live in the future.

IMAGINE THE FUTURE: A LEADERSHIP MUST

Don't let yesterday take up too much of today.
—Will Rogers

Mom answered, "Linda just has a vivid imagination." Mom was trying to dismiss this discussion.

But Aunt Sadie continued: "Why do you want to marry an Indian? Do Indian children go to school around here? Do you have neighbors who are Indians? I thought that the Shoshone Indians were over by Riverton and Lander."

It is puzzling how children get ideas that seem so remarkable at the time. I had never visited the home of the Arapahoe or Shoshone tribes; in fact, I knew no Indians. In the rich language environments of the kitchen table, what conversations had I heard that made me select a Native American for a life partner in my future world? Was it even possible to have an interracial marriage in 1949? I am sure that Aunt Sadie thought that I was a weird little girl with long blond pigtails.

Neither of us knew then that I would spend my adult life often in racially and culturally diverse settings. I taught in the Muskogee County Schools in Columbus, Georgia, the first year that the school district integrated the faculty—students were still segregated. My administrative career at Kent State University gifted me the opportunity to travel the world extensively and to host scores of teachers and professors from Africa, Middle East, Eastern Europe. South America, and all parts of Asia at the Center.

Still today, I feel connected to many Native American views on land, including oneness with nature and community. Colleagues often made fun of me when I invited a Navaho elder to give a welcome prayer to greet newly arrived global scholars.

I thought, "Aren't we all visitors to North America? Shouldn't we all be greeted by the indigenous peoples?"

What in my environment inspired these beliefs and feelings? In 1949, Wyoming's law on inter-racial marriages was Wyoming House Bill 153, passed in February 22, 1913. HB 153 prohibited marriages to persons who were "Negroes, Mulattoes, Mongolians, and Maylays." The law did not mention Native Americans. So I guess marrying an Indian was possible.

Like a rancher, in my educational administrative roles I had to deal with the unknown, the future. Ranchers, at first glance, may seem traditional, not forward thinking. Yet, in reality, ranchers had to guess the weather, and adapt when it didn't rain or the blizzard came. Ranchers had to understand national and world events and trends. The price of wool and beef were part of the unpredictability of the future. Ranchers had to follow what happened in Washington, D.C., and the government. The dependency on Taylor Grazing lands and U.S. Forest permits for gazing the sheep and cattle kept ranchers vitally interested in what new policies were being enacted in the Nation's Capitol. Our kitchen table discussions included these topics. Mom and Dad's radio was tuned to the commodities market on the rise and fall of wool, mutton, and beef prices. Future trends were a daily part of my life. These experiences shaped my interest that served me well as a school leader.

Leadership is about change for the future. Leaders must make choices based on what is possible. Leaders must act, move forward to create a new reality, a new future. Good *managers* take pride in being able to adapt to the latest trends. Good *leaders*, shaped by visions of what the future could be, are eager to make the decisions that help shape the future. Were Dad and Mom teaching this to me in some way? Were the decisions that Dad was making going to predict his future?

An example of this can be seen in one of the last initiatives I led while working at Kent State University. Boko Haram were kidnapping girls from schools in the northern part of Nigeria. American foreign policy and human rights concerns started to intervene in the conflicts involving religions, tribalism, and global warming (reducing grazing lands with the spread of the Sahara Desert). About this time I also served as a regular home host for Global Ties in Akron. Global Ties and the U.S. Government were hosting a group of ministers of education from Northern Nigeria. They asked me if I would host a dinner party for these Nigerian Ministers of Education in my home.

As a result of that dinner party of fresh salmon with these ministers, six months later I received a call from Sokoto's Governor inviting me to go to Sokoto—an arid cattle-raising regions of northern Nigeria. He wanted help in encouraging families to send their girls to school, to improve the quality of teacher's training, and to educate the illiterate women who had been denied education in the past. Dr. Muhammad Jabbi Kilgori, Sokoto Higher Education Commissioner, and my former house guest for the salmon dinner, laughingly called this proposed project, Salmon Diplomacy.

I knew that Nigeria had great assets: the largest population in Africa, a youthful population, oil resources, and was one of Africa's most developed economies. Because of corruption and threats to foreign travelers, few universities were active in Nigeria. However, Kent State University had just honored the Nigerian Minister of the Interior, Lt. General Abdulrahman B. Dambazau as Outstanding International Alumni in 2018.

Even with an invitation from the Governor of Sokoto, the university was reluctant to give me permission me go to this region known for its terrorism. But the little girl with pigtails saw the future with possibilities. Even though I was warned that Kent State did not pay ransoms, I prepared to go with careful planning. As a result of this initiative, about a year later Kent State University was granted a large USAID project of over 3 million dollars to provide educational materials for the schools of the Boko Haram region. Kent State benefitted from visioning possibilities. Seeing the future and being willing to shape that future is a key leadership component.

Watching Dad recruit and plan the brandings, it was natural for me to build networks in my later leadership positions. I agree with Will Rogers, who said, *"A man (or woman) only learns in two ways—one by reading, and the other by association with smarter people."* Being around adults, with more experiences and expertise helped me also to imagine a future beyond Leora's Ranch, beyond what was, and focused on what was possible and likely. Leaders also have to follow Will Rogers' lead, *"Don't let yesterday take up too much of today."* What in your early years shaped your future? Who served you as a mentor?

Chapter Five:

Life Is a Picnic

Aunt Sadie and Aunt Dora went back to Sandusky, Ohio, but summer continued to be fun. After all, Nancy was home from Aunt Vera's for the summer—so I finally had a playmate besides Tippy. The sheep wagon was still parked next to the bunk house. It was now our summer playhouse. Of course, play came in a variety of ways. Mother Nature was also there for us to explore.

Dad always hired young men, usually just out of high school, to work as irrigation and haying hands. These hands stayed in a bunk house just up the lane from our house. Made of wood planks just like our house, it was one big room with several beds, shelves for clothes, a table with a wash basin and bucket of water, and even an electric light for reading late at night. At lambing time it was crowded with the lambing and shearing hired hands. In the summer, just one or two hired men stayed there.

In the summer of 1949, Dad hired Dale Henderson, a recent high school graduate, who became a regular at the kitchen table. Dale wanted to be a veterinarian. Serious about his studies and goals in life, Dale also had a kind heart. One day he found a baby rabbit and brought it to us. Nancy and I fed it, and were amazed at the softness of its fur. Then, as kids do, we decided to give it a bath. We took it over to the irrigation ditch, and stuck its head under the pipe filling the garden's ditch. The baby rabbit fought hard, and slipped out of our hands, and ran away. Maybe a bath wasn't such a good idea. We wouldn't tell Mom why the bunny ran away. And it was a good thing that Tippy was with Dad working cattle that day! He would have chased the runaway rabbit.

That night at supper, Dale asked us, "Where is the baby rabbit?"

Nancy and I looked at each other feeling a bit guilty, and answered simply, "He ran away."

Another time Dale brought a bucket of minnows to us. We spent the afternoon watching them swim around in the water, catching them in our tiny playhouse cups, and then putting them back in the water. This was a treat as we never saw fish in Gooseberry Creek. Dale was teaching us to look more closely at our environment. The next day, Mom made us throw the minnows back in the creek.

Dale found a magpie who was hurt. As he was looking at its wing, he was eager to share what he knew about this fascinating bird, which we often saw and heard at Leora's.

"Magpies are widely considered to be intelligent creatures. Magpies can recognize themselves in mirrors!"

Dale went on, "Some people believe that magpies collect shiny objects such as wedding rings and other valuables. If you see a magpie nest, it will often have shiny objects in it. But they are not good housekeepers like Dot. Their nests are very messy."

The injured bird made a soft murmuring sound—so different from the harsh ascending call we were used to hearing. Dale took the magpie to the bunk house for the night, nursed it for several days, and then let the bird fly away. Nancy and I thought Dale would make a wonderful veterinarian.

Mom, too, was also busy teaching us about nature as we helped her plant and weed in the garden. We were excited when the beans sprouted, the corn showed off with new silk tassels, and the first tomatoes showed red on the vine. Even in the boring process of weeding, Nancy and I noticed the differences in weeds—and weeds seems to grow everywhere.

"What is this one called?"

Mom always knew. "Cheat grass." "Canadian thistle." "Tumble Weed." "Chickweed." And of course, "Dandelion."

English peas were usually one of the first crops ready to eat. Nancy and I would sneak out to the garden to pick a pod or two. Tender green peas. Nothing tastes better! Mom's garden gave us enough to eat fresh in the summer, and she was also able to can some of the vegetables for winter's dinners.

Leora's Ranch gave us a science lesson every day. We heard the meadowlark sing. We knew rain was coming when we could smell sagebrush in the cooler air. We heard the discussion when the bulls needed to be in with the cows. We saw maggots swarming over dead sheep in the hills, and understood the realities of decaying flesh. We saw lambs be born. We marveled over the heart, lungs, intestines, and liver of deer when Dad was butchering. We watched the horses get new shoes, although Dad made us go to the house when he was shoeing horses. He sometimes swore at the horses, and he didn't want to swear in front of us!

In their own special ways, Dale, Dad, and Mom were helping Nancy and me to be keen observers of the world around us.

Developing others seemed natural to everyone at Leora's. Dad and Dale developed a keen bond. During that summer, the kitchen table discussion focused on caring for calves, lambs, and horses. Dad had an eighth-grade education in Gooseberry Creek's one-room school. Grandma Edna Brunk was a teacher before she married, and instilled a love of learning and reading in her children. Dad said he went to the College of Hard Knocks.

Dale and Dad would talk about running a business and developed a friendship that would continue until Dad died. When Dale became a veterinarian, Mom and Dad would go to South Dakota to visit him and his family. Dale often credited Dad for believing in him and being a mentor to him. Dale was just a temporary employee—a high school grad in a summer job irrigating the alfalfa fields. There was no reason for Dad to invest time and effort in him. Yet, Dad saw his potential, and continued to be his friend and mentor.

Later that summer, Dad also hired his nephew, Bobby Brunk, to help with haying. What I remember most about having Bobby around was how he brought out Dad's sense of humor and play. Both were great practical jokers, so we learned to be cautious for surprises. What one didn't think of, the other one did. They loved playing jokes on each other.

Cousin Bobby Brunk, a hired summer hand, later became a scientific rancher using artificial insemination. **Family Photo.**

After that summer of haying, Bobby and Dad developed a special friendship that would last a lifetime. Bobby enjoyed working with animals preferred life on a ranch. This was unlike Dad's brother Carroll, who worked for Standard Oil of Ohio in Grass Creek. Bobby went on to be a successful rancher and brand inspector for the State of Wyoming. He was the one who was among the first to use artificial insemination for his ranch operation on Nowood Creek near Tensleep. Again, Bobby was just a seasonal worker. But Dad and Dale continued a special relationship for the rest of their lives, too.

DEVELOP OTHERS: A LEADERSHIP MUST

If you want to be successful, it's just this simple.
Know what you are doing.
Love what you are doing. And believe in what you are doing.
—Will Rogers.

I share these examples to illustrate how important it is for leaders to develop others—even if the benefit is never felt within the organization. Dad's relationships with seasonal workers could have been much different. I learned from Dad that seeing potential in employees is important and is worthy of mentorship—however, brief. To continue to mentor and stay in touch with promising young people is also the responsibility of a leader.

Developing others is usually not in one's job description. And it wasn't in mine as director of the international center at Kent State University. Yet, Kent State Koleji, a private k-12 school in Istanbul, helped to develop others through an unlikely partnership. And in providing global experiences for those professors who traveled to Istanbul in this exchange, Kent State Koleji helped to globalize the Kent State College of Education, Health, and Human Service faculty.

The school's owner, Talip Emiroglu, wanted an American-style school and wanted an American partner. So an unlikely alliance grew and lasted for years. Kent State Koleji invited Kent State University faculty members to deliver staff development trainings, to consult in designing curriculum and programs, and to help in administrative leadership in Istanbul. In doing so, Kent State University faculty members from various departments within the College of Education, Health, and Human Services traveled together to Istanbul to deliver the training or do consulting work. While not paid for their services, Kent State Koleji covered all airfare, lodging, and dining expenses. So at no cost to Kent State University, the faculty benefitted from a rich, free professional development experience.

Because of this shared travel and work experience, faculty members throughout the college developed a collegiality often not found in higher education institutions—especially across disciplines. This was an added benefit. The week abroad in a Muslim country for these faculty members, living in a modern bustling European city, working in a private K-12 school, and, of course, sharing their expertise in a different cultural setting, all added to the intercultural experience of these mid-American faculty members. These shared experiences, rich in a new culture and in different academic disciplines, helped increase the college-wide commitment to international and intercultural outreach. The fact that Kent State University faculty members were traveling comfortably and frequently to a Muslim country in the decade immediately following 9/11 was a hidden benefit to the institution as well. Over twenty faculty members traveled to Istanbul, and some multiple times with different other faculty in other disciplines. This helped to build a cadre of faculty deeply committed to international outreach, to intercultural understanding, and culturally relevant educational practices. This was a priceless benefit to Kent State University. And yes, Kent State Koleji benefitted from the partnership, too. Classrooms were designed to encourage creativity and play in the early years. English curriculum was modified and improved. Kent State faculty presented faculty inservice on topics like using technology to enhance learning, learning alternatives to the traditional lecture and worksheets, and how to enhance learning for students with special needs. Students and parents from Kent State Koleji came to Kent each summer for a two-or-three weeks English immersion and American cultural experience.

Kent State University did receive a small stipend for the affiliation with Kent State Koleji. Over the years, the number of Turkish students who came to the university increased with exposure to Kent State University and the reputation of the faculty. A simple and unlikely partnership resulted in layers of benefit to the university. Developing others, like Dad mentoring Dale and Bobby, was a natural part of my leadership thinking.

Seasonal hired hands were there because of the irrigation and haying. Yet Dad took time to mentor and continued his relationships with Dale and Bobby long after they left his employment. Leaders know that in developing others, they also change. Continuous learning is vital. Dad mentored Dale and Bobby not because it was part of his job description as the manager of Leora's Ranch. He did it because it was the natural outcome of a code of behavior of developing the next generation. Dad had worked for Mom's father, Charley Schweighart, as a mountain tender for a few summers—he was just a seasonal employee, too. Usually as a young man Dad worked on cattle ranches. But now Dad was managing a sheep and cattle ranch, helped in part from his part-time job working for Grandfather Schweighart. The three years of serving in the Army also helped him gain self-confidence. When the opportunity came, he took a chance at being the boss at Leora's. Now Dad was mentoring others in the same way. It was just the right thing to do.

Ranchers, like other good leaders, know when to stop working, and to take a break from the 24-hour, seven days a week routine that is a part of ranching. This seemed a natural thing to do. In celebration and fun, families on Gooseberry Creek scheduled an annual picnic in late July. This year, as in most years, the Gooseberry Creek picnic would be at the Rankin Ranch, just down the creek from us. Without social media or telephones, somehow the word was spread about the date and time.

On the day of the picnic, we dressed in new clothes Mom had made, and we waited impatiently as Mom wrapped the pot of baked beans in newspapers to serve as insulation keeping them warm. Mom was a genius in finding ways to accomplish what she wanted. When wrapped, the size of the bean packages fit nicely in the box of other items to take to Rankin's. Even today, Nancy and I brag when things always fit together nicely, and say, "We went to the Dot Brunk School of Packing."

But Mom was thinking of the crowds at Rankins' as she finished packing our contributions to the potluck picnic, and turned to Nancy and I. "Don't get dirty before we get there."

Before moving to Leora's, we lived at the Carlson Ranch. We were all getting ready to go to Worland to get groceries and to see our Schweighart grandparents. Mom had Nancy and me all dressed up. Mom stepped out of the house to put something in the truck, and Nancy and I poured lotion all over our pretty dresses. Needless to say, she was not happy with us! Now Mom was warning us! Don't make a mess! We were good, and soon we all loaded up, and went down the Gooseberry Creek Road.

As we pulled into the picnic area near one of the Rankin houses, we saw the gathering under the big cottonwood trees to the south of the house. Tables were spread out, loaded with food for the growing crowd. Scores of women were sitting on chairs around the table, keeping an eye on the food until the bell announced that dinner could begin.

Older men gathered around lazily, some drinking beer, and swapping stories. Others were off to the adjacent field playing baseball. As Dad joined in the game, I watched as Dad hit a big one and ran really fast to first base.

ANNUAL SUMMER PICNIC

This potluck dinner was a gathering of all—no one was excluded. Informal baseball games, abundant food, conversation, and laughter served to bring a geographically distant community to gather with no other purpose—just gather to celebrate community. **Family Photos.**

I was always shy at these events, often hiding behind Mom, and staying close. The crowd of 35 or 40 people was huge and frightening to me. Crowds like this were a sharp contrast to the isolated life I lived at Leora's.

Fried chicken, potato salads flavored differently from every kitchen, wilted lettuce straight from summer gardens, watermelon, pies of every kind, baked beans, and more were laid out in a banquet for the gathered ranching families. Women shared recipes and learned who was expecting new babies. Men complained about the federal government's interference with Taylor Grazing rights, and kids argued over who won the race. Everyone, well, except maybe shy ones like me, seemed to enjoy themselves.

CONNECT TO THE LOCAL COMMUNITY: A LEADERSHIP MUST

Alone, we can do so little; together, we can do so much.
—Helen Keller

However, the annual picnic brought a sense of community, of belonging. The community was formed by geographic dependence on each other in times of need, common challenges, and opportunities. I learned by example that while leadership was needed to save newly born lambs born in a blizzard or to select a good shearing crew, leaders also needed to be part of a community. Organizations or institutions are not isolated. These ranches, remote in geography, were not isolated either.

In each institution where I served as a leader, I worked hard to connect to the local community. One example was the simple decision to connect our global teacher exchange program with the local Rotary Club of Kent. Each year we would take Kent State University international teachers to be the Rotary Club's program for a day by simply having lunch and conversation with the local city and university leaders. We would pair one or two of the international teachers at a round table of six Rotarians. After a brief introduction and the Rotary business meeting, the program would consist of table discussions with the international teachers—very informal, but personal.

David Dix, one of the Rotarians, said, "This is one of our favorite meetings each year. Look at the turnout."

Later when the Covid Pandemic hit in 2021, Rotarians held only virtual meetings, just like the rest of the world. Covid delayed the regular Fulbright teacher exchange, but that did not stop this decade-long affiliation. A zoom meeting connected global teachers from The Philippines, Morocco, India, Uganda, and Brazil with the Kent Rotarians. Once again, the number of Rotarians participating was the highest of the virtual year. Rotarians and the participating Fulbright teachers all learned how different governments were dealing with the world-wide pandemic crisis. In some places where distance learning could not take place because children did not have Chromebooks and internet, children came to school weekly on a schedule to pick up packets of homework. Other countries used nation-wide educational television channels to teach lessons. In other situations, half the class came on alternate days, reducing class sizes to ease the spread of Covid.

Rotarians and international teachers alike all felt a keen sense of common humanity in the shared need to control the virus from spreading. Connecting with this Rotary Club in the beginning was simple. In 2021 the group's most impactful meeting highlighted the shared humanity in the Covid environment.

Connecting with the local community is vital, given the interdependency of humanity today. Leaders and ranchers are not isolated by geography. Staying in touch with the local community is a leadership responsibility.

Mom and Dad always kept the bottom line in their mind, yet they took time for others and to participate in the community. As new ranchers, the workload must have seemed impossible at times, but I never heard them complaining. And they always had time to mentor others, to enjoy a community outing. Will Rogers observed, "*If you want to be successful, it is just this simple. Know what you are doing. Love what you are doing. And believe in what you are doing.*" Mom and Dad enjoyed their life as ranchers. I enjoyed each of my jobs, too. That is the reason I worked until I was 74!

If you enjoy what you are doing, it is easy to connect to your local community. Participating in gatherings as informal as the Gooseberry Annual Picnic helped define a neighborhood spread geographically for nearly 20 miles along the creek bed. Ranchers and their wives had common goals, visions for the future, and a comradery enhanced by helping each other through blizzards and brandings. Leaders who integrate their enterprise into the fabric of the community discover what Helen Keller meant when she said, "*Alone we can do so little, together we can do so much.*"

Dad could have decided not to go to the annual picnic. But could he have recruited as many to help with next years' branding? When decisions needed to be made on the rural electric cooperative lines, would agreement come as easy? When drought made water rights in Gooseberry Creek a concern for ranchers, would those with older homestead dates want to keep the water for themselves? Or would the sense of community take over, with water shared equitably for survival?

In Leora's remote location and its delicate balance of weather and water, Dad and the others knew that the community needed to support and depend on each other. While they competed for the best wool or the best calf crop, they collaborated and cooperated as a community. Dad and Mom didn't have a formal lesson on how to care for others or to connect to the local community. Instead, they lived by a code of conduct that encouraged a natural disposition for these leadership attributes. In what way did your early childhood experiences influence your love for what you do today? In what ways do these experiences help you connect to your community?

Chapter Six:

On the Move

Shortly after being with the crowd at the Gooseberry Picnic and also missing friends from school, Nancy begged Mom, "Can we go play with Shirley and Larry Mullins? Take us there, please."

The Mullins were the ranchers closest to us—up the creek a couple of miles. Larry and Shirley were a bit older than Nancy and me. They were the youngest of the Mullins kids.

Steam was rising from hot water boiling on the stove. Heat showed on Mom's face, as she poured the boiling water over the canning jars. Mom replied with a sigh, "You know that I have to can these beans when they are ready. I don't have time."

Nancy was not to be ignored, "Then can we ride Fawcett over to their ranch?" Fawcett was the old workhorse Nancy and I rode bareback around the ranch.

"No, that is too far." Mom had that edge to her voice that suggested this issue probably was not one to push. And the ranch was almost three miles away.

But she surprised us and said, "Well, maybe we could get word to the Mullins' and the kids could ride halfway, and meet you in the sandstones by the turn in the road." That summer, Nancy was 6, turning 7, and I was 3 turning 4. Mom was pioneering a new way for us to play with friends. She had also been a child on a remote sheep ranch, but she had 9 sisters and brothers as companions. They often played in the hills and canyons by the one-room school called the Schweighart school—mostly all of the students were her family members.

Nancy and I began to jump up and down. "Yes, yes! Tomorrow?? Tomorrow??"

"No. Don't be in such a hurry! I will ask Dale to drive up tonight and arrange a day." Mom was busy putting the snapped beans in the jars. Decisions were made; other important work had her attention. We knew to go outside and play with our stick horses or play pretend in the sheep wagon.

Later in life as a mother and grandmother, I marveled at the fact that Mom had suggested a playdate in the hills via horseback. The sandhill formation was half way between our two ranches, about 1 ½ miles from each of the ranch houses. Maybe she really thought that both she and Mrs. Mullins could benefit from a day without kids underfoot!

Mom packed us a lunch in saddle bags and slung the saddle bags over Fawcett's neck. Fawcett got his name because Dad bought him from Honk Fawcett from Worland. Dad kept it simple when he named horses, Black, Red, Dakota—descriptions of color or purchase place or from whom. That was it.

Nancy used the stump by the house to crawl up on Fawcett, and Mom lifted me up behind her.

As an afterthought, she went to the wood pile, and brought us a hatchet.

"Add this to the saddle bags," she said as she handed the hatchet to Nancy. "This is for the rattle snakes, if you need it."

These hills are half way between Mullins' and Leora's ranches. Mom had pioneered a perfect solution for meeting friends to play. I took this photo in 2021 when I visited the Hillberry Ranch. **Personal Photo**

With that we trotted off in the direction of the Mullins' rendezvous. Tippy didn't go with us. He was tending the sheep in the mountains with Dad.

We arrived at the designated sandstone area, and slid down off Fawcett.

"I smell fire." I said worriedly.

Nancy looked around, then pointed to a blackened area in a tree trunk. "See that! I think lightning must have hit it."

We ran up to it, and felt the heat that was still there. Amazingly, the tree did not actually burn, it was just scorched badly. Luckily, the cedar tree was sticking up out of the sandstone formations so there was not a lot to burn around it, either. We couldn't wait to show the Mullins kids when they arrived.

"Look, there they are," I shouted and pointed west.

We spent the day playing with pebbles as food, stones as play dishes, rocks as rooms in houses, twigs and branches as spoons and brooms. Each of us thought of something different to add to pretend houses and make-believe activities. The day was wonderful. We enjoyed our peanut butter and jelly sandwiches and shared our cookies with the Mullins. Cookies never tasted quite that good when we ate them at home. A picnic in the sandstone hills somehow enhanced the flavor.

There were no adults to organize activities or to say, "No, don't do that!! It's too dangerous!" There was no adult to tell us when to eat our cookies and sandwiches, or in what order. There was no adult to tell us, "Don't get dirty." I remember this day as magical as the fairy tales and leprechaun stories of Pat Mahoney.

We somehow knew it was time to go home. There was no one there with a clock or watch or even an adult's better sense of time. Did the place of the sun in the sky tell us when it was time to go home? There was no one within hearing distance to call, "Come home, now! Time for supper." But somehow we knew.

But first we had another, more important problem to solve. How were we going to get both of us up on Fawcett, the big workhorse? Remember Nancy had mounted using the front steps of the house. Mom had lifted me up behind her. Fawcett, unlike the Mullins' horses, didn't have a saddle with stirrups. Dad would never let us ride with a saddle. He worried that kids might get caught up in the riggings or stirrups.

But just like Mom and Dad when running the ranch, we found our own solutions. Nancy said, "Let's try it on that big boulder over there."

Fawcett, the old compliant horse, moved slowly over to the big boulder. Nancy climbed up on the rock, and then was able to mount Fawcett. Then she asked Shirley to help lift me up behind her, just like Mom had done earlier that morning. Shirley, the tallest of all of us, put her hands out to make a stirrup-like step. Larry boosted me up. And with Nancy's help, I was suddenly up on Fawcett. Larry and Shirley used the same boulder to mount their horses. They each had their own horse and saddles, I jealously noticed! With a wave of hands, and a kick to our mounts, we turned away from each other and headed home.

This memorable day taught me that travel is sometimes necessary to accomplish what you want to do. Mom had come up with an innovative solution. We were rewarded with a day to play with friends and to discover lightning strikes, too!

Leadership training at Leora's Ranch was rich that day and included problem solving, gaining in self-confidence, and even organizing the "work." Going to an unknown place and exploring possibilities was wonderful, and not as scary as a large community picnic.

TRAVEL TO DO THE WORK: A LEADERSHIP MUST

Some people try to turn back their odometers.
Not me, I want people to know "why" I look this way.
I've traveled a long way and some of the rods weren't paved.
—Will Rogers

Later in my life as a director of the global center, travel was part of the job. It was not touristic travel. Travel in this case was travel to do the work. Leadership is about purposing an organization forward. Sometimes to do that, to lead, travel is necessary.

An example of a situation where travel was vital to the success of a project came with our work in Turkey. I was one of the founding members of a development project, Euphrates Tigris Initiative for Cooperation (ETIC). ETIC was formed during the Iraq wars as a Track Two diplomacy project getting academics from Iraq, Turkey, and Syria together to share expertise and data on the two rivers Tigris and Euphrates. Governments were at war in the area, but the water in this arid land was as precious as the water on Gooseberry Creek was critical to our lives—both humans and animals. Water was for irrigating a garden for food during the winter. Water was needed for the alfalfa fields and for the stock to drink. Water meant making a living.

Track Two diplomacy was about interaction and conversations at a lower level than government-to-government diplomacy. The act of having Turkish, Iraqi, Syrian, and sometimes Iranian academics and dam engineers along the Tigris and Euphrates Rivers share information and expertise was the beginning of more meaningful work. This was the preparation for diplomatic meetings for the time when war was over. Sharing water is vital in arid lands whether it be Gooseberry Creek, Wyoming, or Sanliurfa, Turkey.

We held meetings at global events like Sweden's World Water Week and the UN's Food and Agriculture's World Water Congress, as well as UNESCO-financed conferences in Istanbul with dam engineers and academics in water-based development. While the tone of these meetings was usually pleasant and purposeful, over time the management team of Iraqi, Syrians, Turkish, and Americas started to distrust each other due to cultural misunderstandings and a struggle for power within the organization.

Financing agencies like Swedish AID, U.S. Department of State, and UNESCO did not want the project to fail. Dr. Olcay Unver, the project's leader, and I decided that it would be important for me to go to Sweden's World Water Week. My task was to meet with each of the leader members who would also be attending this conference, and try to mend fences within the management team.

In the Arab world, personal relationships are key to building trust. We could not build trust long distance, through emails or even telephone calls. Travel was necessary to bridge the gaps that had occurred and to rebuild relationships.

Face-to-face meetings in Sweden did create hope and a plan for rewriting by-laws. By rewriting by-laws to govern the work, it was hoped that the tensions between founding members would be diminished. If this Track Two diplomacy failed, how could country-to-country discussions ever be accomplished? How could we solve the water crisis in this arid region where water is like gold?

The next step then was to have a meeting in Istanbul, face-to-face, for re-thinking the founding documents. With U.S. Department of State funding, the work session was held. Success was achieved and ETIC continued with new by-laws. Travel for personal contact and to build trust was necessary to save the worthwhile initiative. The playdate in the hills at three years of age was just as adventurous as this high-level diplomatic effort later in life—and both required travel to be achieved.

Community picnics, playdates in the hills, fun hired hands! What a summer! Life was like one big picnic. But summer was not over yet!

Our extended family always came together for Grandmother Schweig-hart's birthday on July 27. Mom's brothers, Carl, Butch, Shorty, and her sisters Myrtle, Sis (Marie), and Alice always gathered with their growing families. Uncle Ed lived in California and missed these family gatherings. This family gathering had almost as many people as the Gooseberry Creek Annual Picnic. But I wasn't as shy because this was family.

All four of us, Mom, Dad, Nancy, and I, crowded into the seat of the Ford truck, bumped down Gooseberry Creek Road or Wyoming Highway 431, and on to Highway US 20 connecting Worland and Thermopolis.

"Mom, sing *'He will not see his mother in the fall,'*" I begged, thinking of Grandma who had lost one of her sons in the Battle of the Bulge in World War II. Mom and Dad often sang during the car rides.

And so Mom and Dad, started the ballad,

"A group of jolly cowboys
Discussing plans at ease
Said one, "I'll tell you something, boys
If you will listen, please."

Pat Mahoney whet my appetite for a story, and this ballad was a story of a cowboy and his mother.

Mom and Dad finished with the final chorus,

"Poor Charlie died at daybreak
He died from a fall
He'll not see his mother
When the work's all done this fall."

I always got tears in my eyes at this part. Wiping my nose with the back of my hand, I said, "Sing it again, please. Please."

Just then we all got distracted by what we were seeing out the windshield. A swarm of people dotted the sugar beet fields along Highway 20. I moved over onto Mom's lap to see better. Wearing hats and bright scarves to protect their faces from the hot sun, men, women, and children were busy bending over in the rows where the sugar beet sprouts were growing.

"What are they doing?" I inquired.

"Those are the Bracero laborers—Mexican workers weeding the beets." Dad answered.

As we drove on, Nancy stretched her neck to see better, too. "Look at the kids…. working in the field, too. They are not bigger than me."

Mom replied and added to the observation, "Yes, and look women with babies in slings are working there, too." We often accompanied her to the garden when she was working there.

Dad responded with a softness in his voice, "I have seen them all crowded into cattle trunks, like this one bringing them from Torrington. It is just a shame to treat people like that."

Torrington was another sugar beet area in southern Wyoming. Our Ford truck was a two-ton truck with a stock rack on it. It could hold lots of sheep or cows. I wondered how those kids felt about having to travel like sheep or cattle crowded in the back of the truck.

Holly Sugar company had a factory on the Big Horn River in Worland and one in Torrington. In 1939, the beet-receiving station at Kirby nearby handled nearly 70,000 tons of sugar beets. This made it one of the largest in the world at that time. To thin the beets in the spring, to pull and cut the tops off in the fall during harvest required lots of hand laborers. During the wartime labor shortage, Mexican laborers helped in the war time harvest. This was part of the Bracero Program started in 1942 as a US-Mexico Farm Labor Agreement. Here in the Big Horn Basin, interned Japanese American volunteers also added to the field hands needed to harvest the beets.

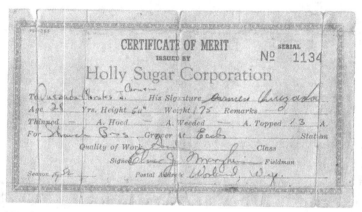

Certificate of Merit issued by the Holly Sugar Corporation to J. Carmen Quezada Morales. It has a serial number of 1134. It lists his age, height, weight, and the work that he performed. The certificate also lists the quality of work as "good". It is dated "1952" and has 'Worland, Wy.' listed as the postal address. **J. Carmen Quezada Morales, "Certificate of Merit," in Bracero History Archive, Item #3013, http://braceroarchive.org/items/show/3013 (accessed May 8, 2021).**

As we drove over the Big Horn River bridge headed into Worland, we saw the small village of cinder block huts where Braceros lived during the summer weeks that they worked in the Holly Sugar company fields. Grass Creek, where Aunt Vera lived, was a company town, too, but it sure didn't look like this one. Instead of the tidy white houses with green shutters in Grass Creek, these huts were just a cement block room. Not all company towns are the same, I realized.

"Where do the kids go to school?" I asked. I wondered if they had to board out like Nancy. Maybe the song about the cowboy who will not see his mother in the fall was still on my mind too. Was I going to have to board out to school, too?

Mom said, "I think they go back to Mexico or Texas in the winter. They don't go to school here."

RESPECT HUMANITY: A LEADERSHIP MUST

I never met a man that I didn't like.
—Will Rogers

Dad ended the conversation as we neared Grace Street, where Grandpa and Grandma Schweighart lived.

"The Mexicans usually stay across the tracks," Dad gestured with his hand as we crossed the railroad tracks into Worland proper. Later I learned that the phrase "across the tracks" would be considered a racist comment.

He went on, "Uncle Frank in Powell has a Mexican couple who have stayed year-round now as field hands, and he says that they are really good workers. Remember the field hand and his wife who were at Uncle Frank and Aunt Josephine's last Thanksgiving?"

But Nancy and I had moved on from this discussion about the Mexican workers. We had just pulled up to Grandma and Grandpa's house. As Dad parked the truck, we leaped out.

We rushed up the back steps, passed the lilac tree, and threw open the back door.

"Hi! Grandma, can we have a cookie?" Nancy opened the bottom cupboard door without waiting for an answer. As she lifted the lid of a large roaster pan, I slid my hand past hers to grab the first cookie. Nancy had one in her hand in seconds, and quietly put the lid back on, and closed the cupboard door. Now that we had our cookies, we knew how to behave.

Grandma always had a roaster full of cookies, stored strategically down low so grandchildren could reach it. Fresh-baked cookies were always there for a welcome treat. In her way, it was our welcome hug.

Grandpa also spoiled us grandkids and would buy strawberries or watermelon as treats for dessert. Cookies were appetizers we could have before dinner!

The trip to Grandma's house for her birthday was also a lesson in respect for humanity that stayed with me in the leadership roles throughout my life. Whenever possible, I tried to design experiences for our global teacher training that taught these highly selected, often privileged teachers from all around the world to respect each other, those less fortunate, and to develop a sense of obligation to improve the lives of all humanity. Every spring semester for thirteen years, we hosted a program titled, International Leaders in Education, sponsored by the U.S. Department of State and administered by IREX, where we brought 20 international teachers from around the world to Kent State University for a semester of academic coursework, internship in public schools, and immersion in American culture.

Although not required by the program standards, we felt that a service component would add to our program. For service, we went to one of our collaborative partners, The International Institute of Akron. Due to the high number of refugees coming into the United States from Myanmar, Syria, and Afghanistan, this non-profit was stretched in their assistance to these newcomers. Since many of our participants were English language teachers in their home countries, we asked if these teachers could help with English classes. The Institute jumped at the chance. Those international teachers who were science, social studies, or mathematics teachers helped to stock the apartments for the refugees arriving at the airport almost daily. By teaching English, making beds, hanging curtains, laying out children's clothes and shoes, and stocking pantries with basic foods items, the international teachers became aware of the way that the United Nations High Commissioner for Refugees (UNHCR) provides official support for refugees globally.

As these international teachers from Ghana, Egypt, India, Brazil, The Philippines, Indonesia, and more countries taught and prepared apartments, they learned about the refugee problems worldwide and started also to think about internally displaced people in their own country's conflicts, as well as victims of tsunami, drought or famine. Rather than just comparing themselves, their schools, their communities to the American life at a Midwestern American university and working in the well-equipped public schools in Ohio, the international teachers were reminded to also think of those less fortunate than themselves.

While Dad and Mom were not helping the Mexican laborers or teaching them English, the conversation in the truck, and Mom and Dad's compassion for the workers made an impression on me. Respect for humanity is not just for those working with refugees or for beet-thinning migrant workers. Respect for humanity is a code of leading that all leaders should have.

As a family we enjoyed travel to play with the Mullins kids, celebrated birthdays, and ate cookies at Grandma's. Mom broke barriers by allowing us at not quite 4 and 7 to be independent. She was not requiring us to be supervised by a responsible adult. Today, in some states she could have been arrested for child abuse. Instead, we learned to be responsible for ourselves, to not be afraid to travel to new areas for great adventures. We solved simple problems like how to mount Fawcett on our own. We discovered lightning strikes and were amazed. Our understanding that travel is sometimes necessary to do work was developed by Mom's willingness and trust in us to be alone for a few hours.

Travel isn't easy even if you don't have a large horse to mount. Will Rogers explained it this way: "*Some people try to turn back their odometers. Not me, I want people to know 'why' I look this way. I traveled a long way and some of the roads weren't paved.*" Certainly Mom was sending us on an unpaved road to play with the Mullins kids. But it was part of the kind of experiences where dispositions for leadership were developed.

We sang with our parents, and learned to appreciate those whose lives did not give us the privileges that we enjoyed. We didn't have indoor plumbing. We lived in a two-room house. We had to haul our own water for drinking and cooking. But we had newspapers to read, a wonderful community of friends, enjoyed Sunday dinner at Grandma's just a truck ride away. Dad was a rancher. We had a good life. The Mexican kids working in the sugar beet fields were not so lucky.

I think Dad would have agreed with our resident philosopher, who said, "*I never met a man that I didn't like.*" In reminding us that Uncle Frank had a Mexican worker with whom we had enjoyed Thanksgiving dinner, Dad was telling us all humans have worth. In his own way, Dad was teaching us that respect for humanity is a leadership must. What in your childhood developed your respect for others less fortunate or provided opportunities to explore the world away from home?

Chapter Seven:

Stepping Up and Stepping Out

Ranch life is not a 9 to 5 job. It is often from sunrise to sundown. That meant in the summer, work days were often long. Dinner might be served later than usual to accommodate the men working in the hay fields or moving the cattle to new ranges. After dinner, we all had to feed the bum lambs in the small pasture by the garden. Mom filled pop bottles with formula and water. Black nursing nipples topped off the pop bottles. Mom handed me only one. Nancy held her hands out for two bottles. Mom, Dad, and sometimes even the hired hands all went out to the pasture to feed the 20 bum lambs from the blizzard. The hungry lambs did not want to wait, so the adult hands handled more than one bottle.

Mom and Dad allowed Nancy and I to choose one lamb to name. I chose the one black lamb, and named him Sambo. Then we were responsible for this lamb—feeding him or her all summer. When the lamb was sold in the fall, the money went to our bank accounts. Dad taught us the value of work and of money you could call your own. Secretly, Nancy and I used to sneak out to the pasture when our special lambs were smaller, grab their wool, swing our legs over, and hop on. We would race through the pasture. Now the lambs were getting too strong, and they bucked us off.

As we walked to the pasture, lambs crowded around the gate. Carefully, Dad opened it, and we all walked into the pasture. Sambo ran to me, nuzzled me, almost knocking me down. I held my bottle carefully with two hands. He found the black nipple, and butted his head against me as he began to nurse. As we were feeding the lambs, Dad said, "Dot, I think that we should go to Grass Creek tomorrow and look at that house."

Nancy and I looked up at Mom and Dad. Nancy quickly asked, "What was that? Look at a house? Were we moving to Grass Creek? "

Well, sort of, I learned later. The next day, we drove to Grass Creek to buy a house for Mom, Nancy, and me to live in during the week when school was in session. Mom and Dad did not want Nancy to have to stay at Aunt Vera's. They heard that a small house was for sale. The location was perfect—right behind the general store owned by Roy Williams, Dad's nephew. Roy was also the postmaster for Grass Creek. Dad's brother, Carrol, owned an interest in the tavern located across the road. Several other small homes and a tent dotted what might be called the town center. Mom and Dad quickly saw that this was perfect place for us. The school bus stopped at the general store.

A mile or so east of the general store, the company community was defined by a fence and looked starkly prosperous. Owned by Standard Oil of Ohio (SOHIO), later called Marathon, the houses' green roofs and white shingled sidings looked crisp and clean. The fenced-in community also featured a large bunk house for unmarried men, a separate cook house, and another building that had been a hospital before everyone had cars. Green lawns, a luxury in the arid Wyoming steppe, made the SOHIO area look like an oasis in the desert. The community was bustling with activities organized by the residents— a Women's Community Club, Girl and Boy Scouts, 4-H clubs, as well as Sunday schools and church services.

The Grass Creek oil field was one of the most active in Wyoming. The landscape around the Grass Creek community was dotted with many drilling rigs. The current drilling boom brought mobile homes to Grass Creek. A village of mobile homes set up outside the SOHIO fence for the rig workers and their families. Grass Creek School, further up the road, had its own oil well on the playground, three teachers, and a principal. Grass Creek was in the middle of nowhere, but it didn't have the feeling of solitude like Leora's.

Standard Oil of Ohio (SOHIO or Marathon) started a company town at the Grass Creek oil field as early as 1917. This tidy little community featured grass lawns and swings for children. **Photo courtesy of Hot Spring County Pioneer Museum and Cultural Center, www.thermopolismuseum.com.**

After living in the small two-room house on Leora's, a three-room house with neighbors seemed really exciting. "What a mansion." I thought!

Now we had a living room, running water in a sink in the lean-to porch, gas cooking and heating stoves, and a delightful pie-cooling shelf in one of the kitchen's windows. The two-hole outhouse even had a small gas heater to keep the users warm in the winter. We learned later that natural gas was free to residents as a community gift from Standard Oil of Ohio. Out buildings also included a garage for a car, and small chicken coop with small fenced yard.

Our newly purchased house (some might have called it a tar paper shack) and out buildings were painted with a special silver paint. The flaring of natural gas as part of the drilling process from the wells owned by Standard Oil produced black carbon and methane gases. These gases made the paint peel off houses unless the house was painted with special paint—thus we had silver paint on the tar paper covering. The Grass Creek SOHIO houses had manufactured shingles so they always looked white, tidy, and beautiful.

To my delight, the other neighbors had kids! The Williams cousins, Laura and Susie, lived behind the Country Store and were really too young to play outdoors alone. Two boys who lived in the other houses, Curt Kuberry and Randy Kruger, were exactly my age. Curt's dad worked for the Platte Pipe Line, and Randy's dad worked for the LU Sheep Ranch further up the Grass Creek Road. I thought that we were really moving up—playmates!

But I wasn't entirely happy. I asked Mom, "Why do I always have boys to play with, but no girls?"

When we went to Grandma Schweighart's, cousins my age were Don Pitt and Leslie Davis. Cousin Joyce Pitt was Nancy's age. When we played with the Mullins kids, Nancy had Shirley, and I had to play with Larry. Now the two boys who would be available to play during the school day were Curt and Randy. Curt had an older sister, Pat, but she would be in school! While I complained, I later found that being around so many men and boys was a blessing.

I was always comfortable being around men working. Here I am helping Uncle Pat feed calves. **Family Photo**

At the kitchen table at Leora's, we were always eating with two, three, or even ten men. Pat Mahoney, the sheep herder and storyteller, was my friend and mentor. The summer hands like Dale and Bobby were part of my daily life. I often spent the day watching the men at work—shearing, docking, and working on the Ford tractor.

I don't have memories of sitting in the kitchen watching Mom bake or cook. Mom and Dad were partners in decisions and each valued the work and knowledge that the other brought to the ranch's success. I didn't have role models of women in non-traditional roles. But I did have the support to dream big, to be anything I wanted to be, even a rancher.

I didn't grow up to be either a rancher or a rancher's wife. But I did become the first woman principal of an elementary school in Portage County, Ohio, in 1978. I was also the first women principal of a secondary school in the same county years later, and thus was also the first woman administrator who had to attend the athletic league meetings with all the male athletic directors and other male principals. Title IX hadn't really kicked in for the administration of women's sports. As a school administrator in these years I was working in a man's world. At state and national conferences, there would be only a scattering of women. I was often asked to present about women's leadership issues at the National Association of Elementary Principals and at local university administration classes. Later on, I was the first woman principal to be named Ohio Secondary Principal of the Year. Did my experiences at Leora's pave the way for me?

PAVE THE WAY FOR OTHERS: A LEADERSHIP MUST

Referring to Nellie Ross, first woman governor in the U.S. and the first woman director of the U.S. Mint.

Nellie's management style was characterized by close personal relationships with some of her subordinates and an integrated approach to her staff as a whole. She demonstrated that she was concerned about and interested in their personal lives, not just their work productions.
—Treva J. Shee

I am always proud of the fact that I was born and educated in Wyoming, the Equality State. Wyoming was the first state to give women the right to vote, and the first state to have a woman governor. My early experiences at Leora's rooted me in a man's world. It was easy for me to read the literature on leadership from business and even military sources. My leadership style was always collaborative, intuitive, and rooted in much of the feminist leadership theory. I now know that, although I never identified myself as a feminist leader. However, my friend and researcher on dispositions of leadership, Dr. Cathy Hackney, tells me that feminist leaders focus on awareness of self and others, developing social consciousness and courage. Feminist leaders lead with soul. I think I have done that, and urge men and women leading educational institutions around the world to do so, too. With the focus on the future, having empathy, caring for others, and developing others were all part of my early childhood experiences at Leora's. Growing up in a man's world was in some way a gift that made opportunities for me in the future. It gave me the confidence and comfort to be myself.

As a family we were stepping up with the purchase of the house in Grass Creek, and stepping out of the remoteness of life at Leora's. But we also enjoyed a large extended family of aunts, uncles, and cousins in Grass Creek and the Big Horn Basin of NW Wyoming. The extended family was scattered in all directions, and we did take time to visit them.

Dad and Mom were close to Aunt Josephine and Uncle Frank, who lived in Powell, and grew sugar beets. When Dad returned from the war, Uncle Frank hired Dad as a seasonal employee. Powell was the first place Mom and Dad lived on their own, and where I was born.

To go to my Aunt Josephine's house, we had to pass the ruins of the Japanese internment camps at Heart Mountain near Cody. Created by Franklin D. Roosevelt's Executive Order 9066, Heart Mountain Internment Camps housed 10,767 Japanese Americans from 1942-1946. Living in the harsh conditions of tarpaper shacks, these Japanese American citizens were treated more like prisoners or war criminals than as citizens. By law these citizens could not be forced into labor, but many volunteered to help the war effort by helping to harvest sugar beets for the Holly Sugar Company in the Powell and Worland.

Photo of the construction of the camp in 1942. **Photo from *Remembering Heart Mountain: Essays on Japanese American Internment in Wyoming*, Edited by Mike Mackey, A Western History Book Publication, 1998.**

Japanese arriving in 1942. **Photo from *Heart Mountain, Life in Wyoming's Concentration Camp*, by Mike Mackey, A Western History Publications Book, 2000.**

As we drove by, Dad looked to the west to the remains of the camp.

His voice had a catch in it, and he said quietly, "Isn't it a shame that our government did that to American citizens? They were not the ones who bombed Pearl Harbor!"

Dad had served in the Army in the Pacific War against the Japanese, and yet he was sympathizing with the Japanese families who had been interned here for four years.

Only a few Japanese Americans stayed in Wyoming after the internment was over. Some became truck farmers growing vegetables and fruit. When the cantaloupe season was in at their farmer markets, we often stopped to support them. Dad appreciated the Japanese work ethic, their polite and respectful manners, and the fact that they were good business people. In contrast to this view, my Aunt Alice Beckley reminded me recently in a conversation about the Japanese internment camps that many people in Worland were not happy when Japanese Americans bought land and became local residents.

HONOR HUMAN RIGHTS: A LEADERSHIP MUST

We will never have true civilization until we have learned to recognize the rights of others.
—Will Rogers

Dad and Mom were setting a tone of empathy and understanding that would serve me well as a leader. Later in my professional life, I learned that racism or conversely, acceptance of others, is formed early by what happens around, with and to children. Empathy does not occur automatically. It requires experiences and reinforcement. I learned to read Mom and Dad's feelings through their actions, responses, gestures, tone of voice, and facial expressions regarding the Japanese Americans and the Mexican Braceros!

Empathy is complex. Cognitive empathy is the sense of "walking in the other's moccasin." Emotional empathy is to be able to understand the feelings that others might have. Behavioral empathy is the ability to change your own behavior to connect with the other. I did not have the opportunity to interact with people different than me. But I started to develop both emotional and cognitive empathy from the actions and discussions in the car as we traveled throughout the Big Horn Basin to Grandmother Schweighart's in Worland and Aunt Josephine's in Powell.

Certainly even this limited intercultural experience served me well in my career later. I traveled, lived, and studied in over 40 countries. I directed development projects and conducted study tours in Asia, Europe, Africa, South America, and North America.

Many times I have been the only woman, or the only American, or the only white person in situations. Having lived in an area where most everyone was like me, how did these brief encounters in the car with my parents help shape my acceptance of others?

In the ETIC project mentioned earlier, I was often the only American. At one conference with dam engineers from the four countries—Iran, Turkey, Iraq, and Syria, I was one of few women on a transport bus taking us all from the training site to dinner on the Bosporus in Istanbul.

One of the Iranians turned around in his seat, and asked me, "Dr. Robertson, do you think that Iran should have nuclear power?"

All of those on the bus suddenly were quiet. I thought carefully before answering.

"Some of the electricity to light my house in Ohio comes from nuclear power. You should be able to light your house as well."

Everyone laughed, including the Iranian dam engineer who asked the question. We went on laughing and talking about the sites along the Bosporus. I think this was use of the emotional empathy that was developed in the early years at Leora's Ranch. I was connecting with him personally and answered in that way. I ignored the nuclear weapons issue that he was probably expecting.

Another time while working on this same initiative, I was invited to attend a Food and Agricultural Organization of the United Nations seminar on the food shortage in the Nile River Basin in Africa. I was the only American, white, and female. I was there as an observer to learn about international collaboration of a river system to help the ETIC project.

One night at dinner, seated at a large table of African men from Egypt, Sudan, South Sudan, Yemen, Ethiopia, Somalia, Kenya, and Uganda, one asked me. "Who is going to win? Obama or Clinton?"

I am sure that the man who asked the question thought that I would say "Clinton." As a woman, I would favor another woman. But I remember thinking quickly, and thought of what was happening in many of the countries represented at the table. When a leader was in power, often that prime minister or president tried to stay on forever. Here was an opportunity to talk about an important part of democratic governing. Always the teacher, I was going to use this opportunity to set an example.

So I answered this way. "Obama will win. Americans don't want Bush, Clinton, Bush, Clinton. The American people are more ready to have a black president than to keep the same families in power."

Little did I know at the time that Obama would win. To answer this question, I was using behavioral empathy. This was a teachable moment in my eyes, and I used this opportunity to talk about the values in democracy. The empathy developed for others from the road trip conversations in Wyoming helped to shape my leadership style in diverse settings.

While sheep shearing, branding cattle, and bum lambs had been my only existence for the first months at Leora's Ranch, my world was widening. I was stepping up and stepping out. Leadership training continued in the years split between Grass Creek and Gooseberry Creek. A widening world is part of that leadership training.

In a wider, more inclusive world, leaders like Barack Obama must pave the way for others. Proud of Wyoming's Equality State status, I always was proud that Nellie Ross was the first woman governor in the United States and the first woman director of the United States Mint. Trave J. Shee, in her book about Nellie Rose, said, *"Nellie's management style was characterized by close personal relationships with some of her subordinates and an integrated approach to her staff as a whole. She demonstrated that she was concerned about and interested in their personal lives, not just their work productions.*" In doing so, Nellie Ross, was paving the way for others. As the first woman in several different categories, I also paved the way for other women.

Today's diversity requires leaders to respect human rights, including those of women globally. Respecting human rights and knowing the United Nations Declaration of Human Rights as a charter should be a requirement for all leaders. Whether a leader is running a small business, a school, or working in a large corporation or university, respecting human rights should be at the forefront of the leader's decision-making. Will Rogers hits it on the spot with this quote: *"We will never have true civilization until we have learned to recognize the rights of others."* What in your childhood helped you to develop empathy for others? In what ways have you paved the way for others? Are you familiar with the United Nations Declaration of Human Rights, inspired by Eleanor Roosevelt's work?

Chapter Eight:

Igniting Sparks

The summer's social season was closed officially when ranchers and town people alike gathered together for the Meeteetse Annual Labor Day Rodeo. Labor Day marked the beginning of school, busy harvest, and trailing cattle and sheep down from the mountain. The Meeteetse Rodeo activities started early downtown with the annual Labor Day Street Races. The races were run in the street by the Meeteetse Mercantile building. Races by age group, three-legged races, and races for cowboys with spurs on were all part of the fun. BBQ beef was simmered under hot coals in the nearby park, sending mouth-watering aromas through the cheering crowds.

"Can I run a race, Mom? Can I? Can I?" I begged, knowing that if I could ride Nancy's stick horse, I would most certainly win.

"No, it is just for school-aged kids," Mom responded squelching that idea. I looked at the next group of runners getting ready at the starting line. Wasn't that Dad?

"Look, Dad is in the Cowboy Race!" I shouted. I moved around to be in front of Mom for a better place to watch Dad.

The gun went off, and the cowboys broke into a run faster than quarter horses. We all cheered.

"Come on, Daddy!" I called him that when I really wanted something.

"You can do it, Lee!" Mom was cheering for Dad, too.

And would you believe it! He won! "See all of us are fast," I thought, reflecting on how fast I was when riding Nancy's stick horse. I was so proud of Dad.

After eating BBQ beef and baked beans, we went to the rodeo grounds to watch the rodeo. Dad had entered the calf roping. He roped calves at the brandings and on the range, but this was the first time that we saw him in a rodeo. The saddle bronc competition was the first to entertain the crowd after the singing of the National Anthem. The flag was held proudly by girls on horseback. Next came the bareback riders—Dad had been a saddle and bareback rider as a younger man.

"When is the calf roping?" I asked Mom.

I was hot, dusty, and tired of the crowds. I was bored sitting still for so long. Broncs, some with saddles and some without, were bucking off cowboys. When was it time for Dad's calf roping?

When the calf roping finally came, Dad chased the calf half way across the arena, but he caught it. He jumped off his horse, and had some trouble getting the calf thrown to the ground to tie its legs up. But he eventually threw up his hands. Done! That was it? It is already over?

"Did Dad win?" I asked Mom knowing that he was a winner! Didn't he win the race this morning?

Calf roper at Meeteetse Labor Day Rodeo, probably Dad. **Family Photo.**

"No, he took too long. It was a big calf." Mom sighed in reply knowing that it took a lot of practice to be a good rodeo calf roper.

After a day of races, BBQ in the community park, and watching the rodeo through the dust, I was ready to go home. But home now was in Grass Creek because Nancy would have school the next day.

I fell asleep as we drove back to Grass Creek to our new home. In the decades that followed, Dad always spent Labor Day at the Meeteetse Rodeo. He never raced again. But Dad improved his calf roping, and later started team roping. I am sure that he was a winner there as a roper, not just a runner in the cowboy races. For our family, the Meeteetse Rodeo marked the end of summer!

Life in Crass Creek was the beginning of a new life. Nancy walked to the front of the General Store and caught the big yellow school bus. Mom waved goodbye to Nancy, and was relieved to know that the purchase of the house was allowing her to see Nancy off to school. Mom smiled at how pretty Nancy looked in her new dress. Mom had finished making it just last week. But Dad didn't get to see Nancy off to school. Mom was with us kids, and Dad was back at the ranch.

BE PROACTIVE: A LEADERSHIP MUST

Even if you're on the right track,
you'll get runover if you just sit there.
–Will Rogers

Mom seemed to blossom in this new small town—she volunteered to be a Girl Scout leader, even if Nancy and I were too young to be members of Girl Scouts or even Brownie Scouts. I remember listening to the Girl Scout Badge work –how to take care of a burn (always a concern of SOHIO for its men in the oil and gas fields), how to make a bed, and learning the names of birds and trees in nature. This was like pretend school in the sheep wagon. But Mom knew more than Nancy!

She took her troop for outings to her childhood home at the Schweighart Ranch on Cottonwood Creek and to Aunt Vera's log cabin high in the mountains on Wood River. The troop stayed overnight at Grandpa's first log cabin on the homestead—Nancy and I weren't allowed to go with her. We stayed with Aunt Vera. But we went on the hikes for the Wood River outing, as you can see in the photo. I am second from the left.

Mom's Girl Scout outings like this hike to Aunt Vera's cabin on Wood River gave Nancy and me enriching activities. **Family Photo.**

Mom also took a Red Cross first aid course taught by the Hot Spring County Health Department at the old hospital at the SOHIO camp. She volunteered with the parent teachers' association at school to help plan the upcoming Halloween community party. She also started to bake pies for sale at Roy's General Store. A piece of Dot's rhubarb custard pie and a cup of coffee was the treat of choice when the local citizens stopped by the post office to pick up their mail or to buy a half gallon of milk. Mom and Dad were always entrepreneurial and knew how to make an extra buck!

Dad and Nate Brown started the first-ever Grass Creek roping and riding club to practice calf roping and other horse-riding games. Mom and Dad were setting excellent examples by their involvement. They were seeing opportunities and then doing something about it—with the hospital closed, first aid trained people were valuable in a community. With rodeo becoming more competitive with increased participation, small roping clubs would help young people compete. Girls Scouts would help young girls earn badges in cooking, first aid, camping, and leadership. New to the community, Mom and Dad jumped right in and created sparks for a brighter future.

Creating the spark for a better future is not complicated. You just have to do it! In my work at Kent State University, the Gerald H. Read Center for International and Intercultural Education had a reputation for innovation, for creating the spark. At the height of the Syrian and Myanmar refugee crisis, the unpopularity of immigration policies caused uproar in many Ohio communities. How could the schools handle all these non-English speaking students? Students with interrupted schooling were coming into the secondary schools barely able to read or write. School leaders were asking Kent State University for help.

In conversation with Dr. Bill Hiller of the Martha Holden Jennings Foundation, Bill lit my fire to do something about the issue of refugee children in Ohio schools.

Bill reminded me, "We have to remember that Ohio is a border state, too. Canada is just across Lake Erie. We don't have to go abroad or cross an ocean to do international work."

That made me think of the possibility of taking Ohio teachers and administrators to Canada in order to learn how they were integrating the influx of refugees. In the news, it seemed that the Canadians were doing this so much better than the United States.

With funding help from the Martha Holden Jennings Foundation, we started to take groups of educators into Windsor, Canada, a three-hour drive away, to learn from our neighbor to the north. This was innovative thinking— we sometimes forget what is right in our own backyard. Everyone thinks Canada is just like the United States. But most don't know that Canada doesn't have a federal system of education, and that each province has its own education laws. Ontario operates four independent public systems—a French-speaking Catholic public school system, a French-speaking public school system, an English-speaking Catholic public school system, and an English-speaking public school system. Windsor, right across the Detroit River from Detroit, also had an Arabic language immersion public school in the English-speaking public school system. In Ohio, we were worried about how to integrate non-English speakers into one public school system! Ontario to the north had as many if not more refugees and had to deal with four public school systems!

Kent State University sponsored a series of two-day trips from Cleveland to Windsor to study and learn from the Canadians on ways to fully integrate the non-English speaking refugee children. Teachers from Painesville City Schools in Ohio, with 40 percent Hispanic population, were the first to go, and the one school district that followed the Canadian models the closest by integrating all social services into the school setting. With many undocumented parents, the one governmental agency they trusted was the school educating their children. If other services could be housed there, they would use them. This benefitted the children, who were often fully American citizens. The answers, or at least the inspiration for solutions, to problems may be found if one is observant and aware.

Mom and Dad served as catalysts by assuming leadership roles in the Grass Creek community. This continued for the rest of their lives. In fact, Dad was honored as Man of the Year in the 1980s by the local chapter of Veterans of Foreign Wars for his work with the youth in the local high school rodeo club and the Hot Spring County Fair Board. Mom was a volunteer in many ways throughout her life, even serving as the volunteer host for the exercise club at her senior living home in her 90s. Leadership training is often as informal as setting an example.

The school years of 1950-1951 and 1951-1952 are fused in my memory. The routines of Leora's spring time activities like lambing, docking, shearing, branding, and summer activities like the Gooseberry annual picnic. Grandma's birthday, and Meeteetse annual rodeo were the same as previously shared. Perhaps bored by routine, I started a new campaign. But I was having trouble igniting any fires with this one.

TAKE CHANCES: A LEADERSHIP MUST

You've got to go out on a limb sometimes
because that is where the fruit is.
—Will Rogers

I started to nag Mom and Dad about adopting a Korean orphan. Somewhere, I am not sure how, I learned about Korean children left on the streets to fend for themselves. I am not sure how much of the news I understood at that young age. But I do remember thinking that there were Korean girls and boys who were not wanted.

I lived in very modest conditions, but the conditions for these children were deplorable. I was never hungry. I always had a good place to sleep. I always had appropriate clothing for the harsh winters. We did not go to church or Sunday School, so I was not influenced by a Christian community's involvement in this large international adoption initiative. Nor did I know anyone who had adopted a child from Korea. In fact, in double checking dates when many American families adopted Korean orphans, the date was later than I remember. Usually the children up for adoption were biracial. I did not have this image in my head. I just remember nagging Mom and Dad persistently during the years in the Grass Creek house.

I begged Mom and Dad to adopt a Korean boy to help Dad. "Mom, Dad needs a boy to help on the ranch. Can't we please adopt a Korean boy?"

Mom, trying to deflect me from this outlandish thought, replied, "It is too expensive to raise children. We have two. That is enough."

She had been raised in a family of 11 where Grandma had raised nine to adults. Dad was from a family of six. Mom and Dad knew the costs of large families.

"But Mom, Dad needs a boy, and wouldn't it be fun to see a Korean boy in a cowboy hat!" This was a conversation that we had over and over. I nagged.

I tried to convince my parents, but they never showed an interest. I do not have a Korean brother. But Mom and Dad did not make me uncomfortable about my wish for a Korean brother, either. They brushed it aside, but never said negative things about the idea.

Oh, well. Mom diverted my attention on adoption, and turned it to a seasonal holiday. Halloween was coming up and for the first time we were going to celebrate. On Gooseberry Creek, ranch houses were too far away for trick-or-treating. Now Mom and others were excited about the upcoming Halloween party at the school. Mom bought a rubber pull-over mask of a man smoking a cigarette. With Dad's hat and clothes she really looked like an old ranch man. For me, it was too scary. Nancy and I dressed more simply. We were ghosts, pulling old pillow cases over our heads with holes cut into them for our eyes and noses.

On Halloween, we entered the gym of the school all decorated with orange and black crepe paper. Everyone was dressed up. You couldn't tell who was who. I held Mom's hand tightly–too scared to turn loose. Who was that man dressed up in a grass skirt, black on his face, and a bone on his upper lip! I hid behind Mom.

Adults and kids played games. Prizes were won for costumes and games! Eventually masks came off so cupcakes and popcorn balls could be eaten. It seemed like everyone had fun, but me. I really didn't like Halloween. It was too scary. I hadn't been afraid of Pat Mahoney's tales of fanciful leprechauns and fairies, but seeing Halloween masks and skeleton figures was uncomfortable to my already imaginative mind. My first Halloween was not a fun one!

In the years since, I learned to embrace the spirit of Halloween, and enjoyed helping my students and daughter prepare for the celebration. Halloween's popularity also grew globally. At Kent State in the spring semester, the International Leaders in Education Program exchange teachers were disappointed that they weren't going to experience Halloween. As English teachers, most of them wanted to celebrate Halloween. One group nagged, like me wanting to adopt a Korean child, but were more successful. Unlike,

Mom and Dad, I gave in. Yes, I would host a Halloween haunted house at my home even though it was March. We asked their Friendship Families to help the international teachers make or find costumes.

The night of the party, Kent State staff members drove most of the group of 22 to my house, but we needed to hire an Uber for the last four guys. The Uber was a bit late, so the four guys were alone when they were picked up. The driver, already knowing the address, quickly turned into the street. The apartment complex where the international teachers lived was right across from the city police station. As the car pulled quickly into traffic, the police lights and sirens started. The driver pulled over. He thought, "I wasn't speeding. I was just turning into traffic. What's up?"

The international teachers all dressed up in masks and costumes were in the car as the policeman came to the driver's open window.

"What is going on here? Where are you going?" demanded the policeman.

Mohammed, taking the lead, responded "We are going to a Halloween party."

"It is March! There are no Halloween parties in March. Maybe you are getting ready to rob a bank! Let me see your identification," barked the policeman.

The international teachers had names like Mohammed, Mustafa, Ismail, and Ahmad and only had Kent State ID's. They had no driver's licenses with local addresses. Passports were in their apartments for safe keeping. This just added some complexity to a situation that neither the driver nor the international teachers understood—why were they stopped?

Let's just say that it took some fast talking, and a phone call to me verifying that these men were truly coming to a Halloween party in March. The police finally let them go. I guess they finally convinced him that they weren't robbers. For these international teachers, their first Halloween was like my first Halloween—a bit scary.

A leader must be proactive, even if it is as simple as hosting a Halloween party in March! Mom and Dad jumped right in to the communities around us. Will Rogers knows that doing nothing is not an option, *"Even if you're on the right track, you'll get runover if you just sit there."*

Dad won the footrace, and would never compete again at the Meeteetse Labor Day Rodeo Games. But he did move on. He didn't win at calf roping, but started a practice roping club and would continue to rope or teach others until the day he died—literally. (He was planning to rope with a young people's roping club on the day he died of a heart attack at 70).

All of us enjoyed Halloween after that first party. Mom's mask stayed in our family for years, and even I wore it later in my childhood trick-or-treating. The international teachers would talk about their experiences with Halloween in March in the United States, and laugh about it! Mom and her fellow party planners were the sparks for a great night of community fun! Learning from her, I was willing to host a Halloween party in March.

Will Rogers summed it up this way, *"You've got to go out on a limb sometimes because that is where the fruit is."* I tried for several years to convince Mom and Dad to adopt. I don't have a Korean brother. But I never regretted trying. Mom and Dad never rejected me for trying. I spent decades working with international teachers, and still work on refugee issues.

What in your childhood made you willing to be proactive and even risk failure?

Chapter Nine:

Adapting to Survive, Adapting to Thrive

Turning six on July, 15, 1952, I started school the day after the Meeteetse Labor Day Rodeo. After having the freedom to roam all over the ranch head-quarters, school was a radical change for me. I had often been alone as a child. Now I was corralled in a classroom full of kids my own age. Some were ranchers' kids like me, but the majority of the kids were from the Standard Oil of Ohio camp.

Drilling was booming. Many men followed rigs, came and went with their families. Class rosters changed every week. This might have been a problem for Mrs. Weaver, but she handled it well. Mrs. Weaver was my teacher for the first two grades. I loved her and everything about school.

The years of the oil boom in Grass Creek also brought a boom in childhood illnesses. As a kid on an isolated ranch, I worried more about sheep ticks than infectious diseases. But in the early school years, I had mumps, measles, chicken pox, whooping cough, and pneumonia. The oil rig families, moving from camp to camp throughout the state, exposed the ranch kids to all the childhood illnesses. Vaccines for these diseases were not mandated or available.

Measles vaccine started in 1963—I was a junior at Hot Spring County High School then. Mumps vaccines came in 1967—I was a junior at the University of Wyoming. Chicken Pox vaccines were not regularly given until

1995—when I was a school administrator in Ohio. Perhaps having so many of these diseases weakened my immune system, and so I got pneumonia, too.

Mrs. Weaver and her class from Grass Creek School. (front row, far right) I am wearing toe scuffed saddle shoes, jeans, and a cowboy belt buckle, and curly, not braided hair. I am all dressed up for picture day in second grade. **School Photo**.

When I was in Dr. Vicklund's office getting lung x-rays for my pneumonia, I remember him saying, "Yes, Dot, she has pneumonia. Pneumonia is serious. She should probably go to the hospital."

I looked anxiously at Mom, and asked, "Am I going to be crippled?" I was confusing pneumonia with polio, another concern for childhood health at the time. Dr. Vicklund smiled, and reassured me.

Because Mom had taken a first aid course in Grass Creek taught by Dr. Vicklund, he let her take me home. He trusted Mom, but cautioned her to bring me back to Hot Spring County Hospital in Thermopolis if my fever did not break with the antibiotics.

Today's Covid environment reminds us how quickly infectious diseases spread. I experienced that in these early school years at Grass Creek. Mom also learned that childhood illnesses could be prevented. We always got vaccines when they were available. Later, Mom became involved in a volunteer program doing throat cultures for the prevention of strep infections in the Thermopolis City Schools.

SHAPE A BETTER FUTURE: A LEADERSHIP MUST

Always drink upstream from the herd.
—Will Rogers

Throughout this book, I have ended chapters with quotes summarizing the leadership tools described in that chapter. But I am going to break that trend, and insert a Will Rogers's quote that fits our story now. Will's advice to *Always drink upstream from the herd* has a double meaning that fits this discussion. First, let's examine the quote's literal meaning. If a herd was drinking in a river or creek, then humans should always drink upstream. This is common sense. This quote reminds us of safe drinking practices. Remember at Leora's we had to haul all of our water.

When and where water is scarce, hygiene is not always a priority. Some of the practices that we had as a family at Leora's were traditions shaped by the scarcity of water. Childhood illnesses spread at school. But we were also lucky that at Leora's we did not catch other illnesses from some of our family routines.

We—I mean hired hands, gypsy sheep shearers, Cottonseed Jack, and other guests, Mom, Dad, Nancy, and I—all drank from the same ladle in the water bucket! We never thought about it. Because we had to haul water, water was scarce commodity to be reserved carefully. We were not encouraged to wash our hands frequently throughout the day, although we did wash before eating. We didn't bath daily, probably more like weekly. In fact, we all bathed in the same water in a round wash tub placed in front of the stove. When possible, we took baths at Aunt Vera's in Grass Creek. Her Standard Oil of Ohio house was fully modern with bath tubs, washing machine, and running water in the kitchen. We also bathed in Gooseberry Creek in the summer.

Will Rogers's quote is true about hygiene; it is also true of leadership. Leaders must be upstream from the herd figuratively. Leaders need to be ahead of the others. . . being proactive, not just reactive. We were fortunate that Mom was engaged as a volunteer and took an interest in offerings for adult learning to keep up with the medical practices of the times. The fact that she had taken the first aid course probably kept me from the hospital. Her actions were proactive. She made sure that we got a sugar cube with the polio vaccine when it became available. She was being proactive.

While some of our home routines were tailored by custom and scarcity of water, Mom worked at keeping us clean and healthy—in her own way she was proactive. Both Mom and Dad were raised on Big Horn Basin ranches where water was scarce. Even with good water wells, water usage was hampered by that fact that someone had to go to the well, pump it by hand, and haul it to the house.

Later as director of international programs, I also had to think how to drink upstream from the herd. For example, once I had to be the one upstream from two angry international exchange teachers. The two, roommates one from South Africa and the other from Ghana, came into my office. I could tell they were clearly angry.

"Good morning! You two seem upset. Need to talk?" I inquired.

The South African demanded with pointing finger wagging, "I can't live in these conditions! It is just unhealthy! I am just so angry because she does not put the dishes away after using them. They are left all over the counter, in everyone's way, messing up the apartment, and getting dirty from being out!"

Her Ghanaian roommate could hardly wait to tell her side of the story. "Dr. Robertson, she wants me to use a dirty old towel to dry the dishes! Who wants to eat on the dishes after she wipes them dry with a dirty old towel?"

Secretly, I wanted to laugh. This was a roommate fight over *clean* dishes! I dealt with lots of roommate problems in these international teacher exchanges. One of the requirements was that exchange teachers had to room with someone from another country. But I never had to deal with a fight over *clean* dishes!

"Explain to me why you both are upset." I needed to listen, then act proactively.

The South African had been taught to wash, then dry dishes with a clean dish towel, and to put the dishes away as soon as possible so that they would stay clean. The Ghanaian had been taught to wash the dishes, and then let them air dry. A dish towel might not be clean, and should not be used. She would spread the dishes including pots and pans all over the counter to dry. Probably, there were a lot of other little things, like missing their families and their homes, added to the conflict, but I was trained to deal with one intercultural misunderstanding at a time.

As I leader, I had to find a solution that would satisfy both. I bought them a dish drain rack, and asked them to use this. Then as soon as the dishes were dry, each were to put them away in the cupboard. In this way, no towel would be used. Air drying would be the method, but the dishes had to be stacked in the rack, and not left out all over the counter. They agreed to try this.

Leaders need to know when to take even small things seriously, and handle them with respect. At Leora's, we felt fortunate to have water to wash the dishes! Geography dictates practices even in dish washing. Proactive learning, proactive actions, and thinking ahead are key leadership components. With its closed windows and longer days inside, winter might have been bad for our health, but it was also special in other ways.

With no garden or farm chores, Mom had less to do in the house in Grass Creek with just the two of us. She had time to read to us every night from the Tracy Belden and the Bobbsey Twins series, as well as other favorites. We had a few books and brought more home from school. My favorite was *Tommy of the A Bar A Ranch*, a story about a boy who saved a calf in a snow storm. Can you see why I could relate to this story? I made Mom read that book over and over until the pages started to fray.

Christmas was coming, and in Thermopolis, children could have the photos taken with Santa Claus. This sounded exciting to Mom so she asked, "Do you want to go to town and see Santa?"

"See Santa? Before he brings us Christmas presents?" Nancy inquired with a frown on her face.

"Yes, you can tell him what you want, and then he will bring it on Christmas Eve."

"Yes, yes, let's go." Nancy and I yelled in unison, jumping up and down.

Mom dressed us up in new dresses she had made for the holidays. An excellent seamstress, she could even cut her own patterns from looking at fancy dresses in the Sears Catalogues. We were always in fashion, even if our dresses were home-made.

We drove all the way to Thermopolis in the early evening, and went to the Elks Hall. There were what seemed like hundreds of people standing in line, talking excitedly. Kids were dressed up; parents were greeting neighbors they hadn't seen for some months.

Smiling doesn't always mean you are comfortable.
Leaders often have to hide their fears, too. **Family Photo**

When it was my turn to go sit on Santa's lap for the photo, I took one look at him, and hid my face in Mom's lap and started to cry. He was ugly with a funny mask like Halloween on his face. I didn't want to sit on his lap. He was worse than our neighbor, Bill Mullins, who tickled my ribs whenever he came over.

Mom reassured me and after a bit of coaching, I gingerly went over to sit on the edge of his lap for just the second that the camera needed to take the photo. I smiled just because Mom told me to. Then I jumped off.

A couple of days before Christmas, we went to the hills around Leora's to find the perfect cedar Christmas tree. Oh the smell of a fresh cedar in a warm house! That is one of my favorite scents of Christmas—that and Mom baking Christmas ginger double-deckers.

Our holiday tree was put up on Christmas Eve Day to ensure that the greens were fresh. This year for the first time our tree was going to have electric lights! In previous years, we had had candles on our trees. Now the lights could be on for several nights, not just Christmas Eve and Christmas Day. Nancy and I were so excited about this new tradition.

"Mom," I asked for the umpteenth time, "Are you sure that Santa knows to come in the door? We don't have a chimney."

"Yes, Linda, Santa knows that he has to come in the door. He will find you and leave presents."

Mom answered with patience as she tucked us in.

Mom read us the Night Before Christmas poem from the big picture book. Now we were supposed to go to sleep with "sugar plums dancing in our heads." Instead, I was listening for "the prancing and pawing of each little hoof."

I listened. And listened. Couldn't sleep.

I started to cry. "Santa won't come because I can't get to sleep." Mom lifted me up, and sat in the rocker with me. As we were rocking, I listened. I listened. I really could *not* go to sleep. What was that? Was that a door slamming at the General Store?

Was Santa there? I better get to sleep soon. The General Store was close to our house. There was just Al Smith's tent between the General Store and us. I better get to sleep fast.

As I have said before, my mind is always jumping around like fleas on a dog. I stopped to think. Did Santa stop at tents, too? Al Smith, a funny old man in bib overalls, lived in a tent with a sawdust floor. Would Santa visit him? Perhaps he had asked Santa for some shoes as we rarely saw him ever wear shoes. Or perhaps he had asked Santa for a shirt—only in the coldest of weather did he ever wear a shirt. Or perhaps he had asked for a new whittling knife as he was known for his excellent whittling skills. He whittled every day and that is why his floor was filled with saw dust and shavings.

This patten of not sleeping on Christmas Eve would continue the rest of my life! Too much excitement! Or perhaps, I am still listening for Santa.

Santa did come sometime after I finally fell asleep. In the morning, we were excited that Santa had left new dolls dressed in dresses that looked just like the ones Mom had made us for Christmas Day at Grandma's. After breakfast of special cinnamon rolls and sizzling bacon, Mom brushed our curls—no everyday braids for Christmas day. Mom's new tooled leather purse slung over her shoulder. $1 wool helped Santa bring nice gifts.

We were on the road to Grandma's. All the cousins, aunts, and uncles would be there. And more presents. Grandma's presents were always special. She had given us the silver wagon, the one I used for a bed for Pat Mahoney's stories.

Notice I said that we piled in the car. Yes, $1 wool had also paid for a new Dodge car. We were traveling in style now. We had survived those childhood diseases, and now we were thriving!

ADAPT TO CHANGING WORLD: A LEADERSHIP MUST

Things ain't what they used to be and never were.
—Will Rogers

After Christmas, things changed. Mom was tired and losing weight. It was her turn to see Dr. Vicklund. She was diagnosed with thyroid disease, and had to have her goiter removed in the hospital in Billings, Montana.

I remember discussions with Aunt Vera about how Mom and Dad were going to pay for the operation. But thanks to $1 wool they had plenty of money for medical expenses—I don't think they had insurance of any kind. They didn't have to borrow money from relatives to pay for the expensive surgery.

The surgery was out of the state—a long way away! Nancy and I had to stay with Aunt Vera and Uncle Edgar while they were away. Of course, Nancy had been brave and boarded out with them last year, but I just couldn't do it.

"Mom, don't leave me. I don't want to stay with Aunt Vera. Can't I go with you?" I was sobbing.

Mom was emotional too, and (I am sure) worried about the surgery. Tears came to her eyes too, but said sternly, "Linda, you have to do this. Aunt Vera will take good care of you. Nancy will be with you."

With hugs and kisses, she and Dad left. I later learned she cried most of the way to Worland. She was probably also scared of the surgery. She had been in the hospital once before as a teenager with appendicitis. I cried each night that she was gone. I did not like being away from Mom and Dad. And Mom didn't like being away from her children either—hadn't they bought the house in Grass Creek so that the family could be more together?

In a few days, Mom came back with a small scar on her throat, but feeling much better.

Her normal energy returned, and life seemed normal. But other things were about to change.

The three-year lease on Leora's Ranch was nearly up, and Mom and Dad had to decide what to do. Leora wasn't sure if she was going to sell or if George's brother was going to run the ranch. What was ahead for us?

$1 Wool had made Mom and Dad feel that the sacrifices of living in two places, of Dad being separated from us most of the week, was worth it. Now, there was talk of wool prices dropping because war tariffs for wool were being eliminated. The lease was up, and Leora's brother-in-law was going to lease the ranch. Dad had to find another job to support our family.

The $1 wool, his own small herd of cattle, and good decisions gave Mom and Dad some cash. Was it enough to buy their own ranch? They were ready to be settled—they did not want the uncertainty of three-year leases. So our car trips now were not to Aunt Josephine's or Grandma Schweighart's for dinner and fun. Instead, Mom and Dad went looking at ranches for sale throughout Wyoming. One near Moorcroft was too expensive. The one near Thermopolis with the wonderful red hills and amazing two-story house didn't have enough grazing land for even our small cattle herd.

Dad and Tippy moved from Leora's to be with us at the Grass Creek house. At least, it was ours. Several of Dad's favorite roping horses were moved from Leora's to Nate Brown's pastures in Grass Creek. We were adapting to the new situation.

Dad, always a practical problem solver, found some BLM land to lease for his cattle, and started to work in the oil patch on a drilling rig. Rigs operate 24 hours. He was now required to do shift work which meant that he had to sleep in the day. The little Grass Creek house was very hot that summer, and Dad had a tough time sleeping in the daylight. Making it worse, Nancy and I had trouble being quiet enough. Where was our fun-filled Dad? We needed Bobby to be here to liven up the house.

When Dad had a couple days off, he would go to look at another ranch for sale. The number of sheep ranches were shrinking like a cheap shirt in a hot wash. Cattle ranches were too expensive. What to do? It was hard for Dad to accept that his dream of owning his own ranch was out of his reach.

Tippy, our border collie, was unsettled, too. Unhappy being penned up in the old chicken coop at night, and with no stock to work, he simply left the Grass Creek house one day. We looked and looked for him. None of the neighbors had seen him. Was he hit by a car near Roy's General Store? No one reported a dog killed on the roads. Did someone from Tavern across the street take him?

About week later, we heard from some neighbors on Gooseberry, that Tippy showed up at the Hillberry Ranch. He made the decision to stay with the cattle and sheep. He ran through the hills for 20 miles and arrived with sore feet. But for him, Leora's was home.

Dad decided to let Tippy stay. Dad knew that Tippy was a stock dog, and Dad also knew what it was like to leave the ranch life that you love. Dad was starting to think that he wasn't going to have that gift himself. Like Will Rogers, Dad knew that *things ain't what they use to be and never were.* Leaders need to be ready to move on, to adapt to new situations. Mom and Dad were coming to that conclusion. Have you ever been at a crossroads of life, and didn't know what to do?

Chapter Ten:

Moving On

Dad finally settled on a job as a water commissioner for the Hanover Canal Company. The Hanover Canal brought irrigation water from the Big Horn River to Holly Sugar beet growers near Worland. His responsibilities including regulating who had the water when and how much. The Grass Creek house was sold and we moved to the company house at the dam where the Big Horn River was diverted into the Canal. A new Boysen Dam ensured that Big Horn River would be high enough at all times for irrigation water to be diverted into the Hanover Canal for the beet fields near Worland.

The Canal Company agreed to add a huge addition to the house when Dad took the job. Nestled under the biggest cottonwood tree imaginable, the house was under construction. We were used to living in smaller houses, so we adjusted easily to living in the kitchen, bedroom, and porch. Those first summer months, Mom and Dad slept on a bed on the screened-in porch and enjoyed the coolness of it.

A new modern bathroom, large living and dining room, and another bedroom were added. For the first time, we would have our own modern bathroom. No more outhouses. No more hauling water! Two bedrooms? We were not only moving on from ranch life, we were moving up.

The Ditch Camp house was doubled in size just for us! This white shingled house had a cottonwood tree big enough for a rope swing. **Family Photo**.

Headquarters at the "ditch camp" as we called it, also included a barn, a chicken coop, and other little shelters for other kinds of animals. It was like a little town with lots of little houses. I thought the ditch camp was magical and fun! This had been the construction headquarters when the ditch was dug. Thus, we always called this place the ditch camp, like we called the ranch, *Leora's*. In a way it reminded us that these houses were not ours. We didn't own them. We owned the house in Grass Creek, and we simply called it home.

Mom planted a large garden by the house—bigger than at Leora's because now she could be sure to have enough water for all the vegetables. The well here with an electric pump meant that she could sprinkle daily. Mom bought chickens to fill the chicken coop, and sold eggs to our neighbors in Chatham. In the spring Mom ordered tiny baby chicks, so furry and yellow, chirping all the time. They were penned up in another one of the extra little structures at the ditch headquarters. After a few months of careful feeding and growth, all of us were involved in preparing them for sale. Nancy and I had to help with the slaughtering, plucking, and gutting of these young chickens. It wasn't much fun, let me tell you. But these young poulets as we called them were favorites for frying. Housewives knew the poulets were young and tender. Old roosters and hens were better for roasting.

Dad started to train horses. An excellent horse trader, he found partially broke horses, and rode and worked with them to sell at a higher price. Dad bought steers to be fattened and sell for another entrepreneurial initiative. They were supplementing Dad's wages as a water commissioner while still hoping to find a ranch someday.

Nancy and I enrolled in sixth grade and third grade respectively at the one room school house. Winchester School served the small number of families whose fathers worked at the Platte Pipe Line tanks or farmed and ranched nearby. This junction where we lived had two names.

This location where the Cotton Creek Road branched off Highway 20 and midway between Thermopolis and Worland was called Winchester. The name came from the postmaster and local rancher, R.S. Winchester, and therefore was the post office address. Other people called this junction Chatham. Chatham was the name given to the stop on the railroad for freighting iron pipe for oil well drilling at Hamilton Dome and Grass Creek. Mr. Winchester objected to the railroad using his name, and so the railroad used a different name, and the stop on the railroad was called Chatham. How could a junction, with hardly any collection of people, be worthy of two names? This was always confusing to me. As kids, Nancy and I had other things on our minds—like a new school.

"Mom, do you think I will have another girl in sixth grade with me. I don't want to be the only girl." worried Nancy. "I wonder how many will be in my grade? I don't want to be the only sixth grader!"

I disagreed, "I think it would be fun to be the only third grader."

I was more worried about a new teacher. Mrs. Weaver was the only teacher I had ever had. She taught me in both first and second grade.

Neither one of us got what we wanted. Our teacher had three boys. With her three, the number of kids in the one room school was 24. There was someone in all eight grades! Nancy was the only sixth grader. I was one of three in third grade.

Grass Creek was one of the richest school districts in Wyoming because of all the oil. Grass Creek was a modern school with a fenced-in playground and a gymnasium big enough for community Halloween parties. The cafeteria in the basement had a modern kitchen with gas stoves for cooking lunch. The school featured modern girls, boys, and teacher bathrooms at all levels. Grass Creek School even provided cottages for teachers strategically placed behind the school. But the Winchester School was starkly different.

A potbellied coal/wood stove in the corner heated the main school room. In the winter the teacher had to build a fire and keep it going during the day. A cloakroom (who wore a cloak?) was the area where we entered from outdoors, and left muddy from boots and winter coats. Outhouses marked Girls and Boys stood behind the school. And wouldn't you know it that the boys tipped the Girls outhouse as a Halloween prank, and all of the girls had to use the Boys outhouse for a week before the fathers repaired the Girls outhouse! We had to bring our own lunches—there were no friendly cooks or hot lunch program here. Sometimes Mrs. Lewis would put a big pot of soup on the potbellied stove for a treat on the coldest days. The school was painted the same silver as our house in Grass Creek. The gases from the new Platte Pipe Line Oil Tanks next door made the paint peel—even with the silver paint. Mom or Dad had to take us, or we walked the mile and half to school. We had a modern and bigger home, but our school was more like living at Leora's. Were we really moving up?

I loved this one room school because I could do the third-grade work *and* teach the first graders about numbers and how to read. I also liked to listen to what Nancy and the older kids were learning, too. Always an eager and quick learner, I felt I was in all grades at once!

Of course, we didn't think walking to school was too great. One day, we asked to ride our bikes. Nancy broke her elbow falling from the swing at recess, and we had to walk our bikes home. We thought the bikes brought us bad luck, and never rode them to school again. We might have tried to ride horses to school like Dad did, but the school didn't even have a hitching post for horses.

Lucky for us, we only went to school there for a year. In fall of 1954, Washakie County School District decided to close the school. Now big yellow school buses, driven by one of the high school students, drove us the 15 miles to Worland to school. Nancy started seventh grade in a big junior high after being the only student in sixth grade.

LIFE LONG LEARNING:
A LEADERSHIP MUST

Real learning gets to the heart of what it means to be human. Through learning we re-create ourselves. Through learning we become able to do something we never were able to do. Through learning we perceive the world and our relationship to it. Through learning we extend our capacity to create, to be part of the generative process of life. There is within each of us a deep hunger for this type of learning.

—Peter M. Senge

Our second year at the ditch camp, Nancy and I weren't the only ones who started school. Dad decided that he needed to make a change. Mom and Dad got realistic, and decided it was not possible to purchase a ranch with high prices. $1 wool helped the bank account, but that price was now diminished with the wool tariffs changing. Mom and Dad sold the cattle herd. They took their savings and bought rental property in Thermopolis. Dad was adapting to a new economic situation. The rental property was an apartment building with four apartments on a big wide street in Thermopolis, aptly named Broadway Avenue. The second purchase was a small house on Eighth Street. With the refinery and oil fields in Hamilton Dome and Grass Creek nearby Thermopolis was booming. Rentals were always full.

Dad took a correspondence course in air conditioning and heating, and took welding classes at Thermopolis high school's adult education program. Dad completed his courses, and landed a better job with the Wyoming Gas Company as a field hand and welder. We moved to Thermopolis.

After a few months looking for a home, (first we lived in one of the apartments we owned), Dad and Mom bought a house inspired by Frank Lloyd Wright—a much better home than Leora's mice-ridden two-room shack! The house at 813 Mondell was a redwood-sided house with big windows, build-in chests and storage areas, sloping ceilings, natural pebbles on the roof, and the only carport in town. Later after visiting many Frank Lloyd Wright's inspired houses, I realized that the former owners had designed this small house with Frank Lloyd Wright's designs and natural materials in mind. Mom was quick to repaint the black walls in their bedroom. . . she liked some of the modern trends, but not that one! Dad continued to make this house unique when he installed Thermopolis' first solar panel for heat in the 1980's.

Dad's dream of owning a ranch was sacrificed for his family. Our family had endured a lot in trying to make ranching work. Nancy had boarded out to go to school. After we bought the house in Grass Creek, Dad had been separated from the family during the week. At Leora's, we lived in rather primitive conditions. We hauled water. Mom nursed lambs in the kitchen to keep them alive. We bathed in the creek. Dad and Mom wanted a better life. Dad, the traditional bread winner, was willing to start over.

Life is not static. Things change. Times change—the number of sheep ranches in Wyoming declined every year. Lambs and wool had less value. Dad had to change with the times, rethink what to do.

When I was 52, I found myself at a crossroads, too. Our daughter Michelle had completed her MBA degree. My husband Rob's work took him abroad a lot. I wanted to be free to spend more time with him and share some of the international adventures that he was having.

I decided that this was a good time for me to get the Ph.D. that I always wanted. Like Dad, I would retool. So I enrolled at Kent State University. I spent summers and semester breaks with Rob in Europe. In my case, I was fulfilling a dream of working internationally in education while earning a Ph.D.

Starting a new career at age 52 perhaps was not a financial good decision. Public-school administrators received higher salaries than directors of endowed centers in universities. But I held the position of director of the specially endowed center until I was 74 and enjoyed every minute of it. In my career as a public-school administrator in the Aurora City Schools, I used the leadership skills developed at Leora's and by the examples of my parents. Now, I could expand that leadership to a more global outreach.

I met amazing teachers from around the world during that 22-year period in administering programs funded by the U.S. Department of State. Teachers, selected as their nation's best by the Fulbright Commissions in their home countries, came to Kent State to study and learn. I worked with some of the world's best educators—the cream of the crop, as a farmer might say.

I led travel programs and development work in Mexico and Canada, South America, Africa, Central Asia, and Turkey. I spoke at conferences in China, Turkey, South Africa, Egypt, Guatemala, Taiwan, Kyrgyzstan, Germany, Indonesia, India, and Italy. I led travel study programs in Peru, Ireland, Turkey, Bhutan, Nepal, India, and Canada. I gained an understanding of the complexity of intercultural work. I developed an appreciation of the contribution of refugees and immigrants to American society. I went out on the limb, and enjoyed the fruits of my labor of writing a dissertation and retraining when most of my principal friends were counting the days to retirement.

Leaders must know when to renew in today's fast changing world. In previous times, many people had the same job all of their lives. Today's college students know that that continuous learning will be part of their lives—most of them expect to have 6-8 different jobs during their careers.

Leaders also need to know how and when to leave a position. Dad and I could have stayed in jobs as rancher and principal, but the new work was also rewarding. The ability to adapt, innovate, and be successful served both Dad and me well. While this story tells of the leadership training in my early years, I continued to learn through advanced degrees, professional development, reading, and networking. Dad always took classes, too. He enrolled in welding and roping classes, read regularly, and learned from others. With little formal education, he was a life-long learner, too.

Like Peter M. Senge, I believe that leaders need to have a hunger for learning—this is a leadership must. Senge describes it this way, *Real learning gets to the heart of what it means to be human. Through learning we recreate ourselves. Through learning we become able to do something we never were able to do. Through learning we perceive the world and our relationship to it. Through learning we extend our capacity to create, to be part of the generative process of life. There is within each of us a deep hunger for this type of learning.*

In what way are you keeping up with the times?

Chapter Eleven:

Bull Shit with Cream on It

And now we come to the end of this story. I always say I grew up on a sheep and cattle ranch in Wyoming. Yet, the end of this book comes two years after we left the ranch. Dad's transition from ranching, short-term jobs, and frequent adjustments to family life stopped once we moved to Thermopolis.

Tippy ran away and back to Leora's. Dad couldn't afford a ranch. This story of my early childhood experiences seems to end with sad moments. But I don't feel that way. I feel that life has transitions, but that each transition gives new hopes and dreams, new experiences to be cherished and to enjoy. The Frank Lloyd Wright-inspired home was the family home in Thermopolis until Mom moved to Ohio at 85 years of age. Dad retired from the Wyoming Gas Company, and continued his entrepreneurial interests in refinishing antique buggies and trading and training horses. Both continued to be active in the community—bowling on leagues, serving youth as leaders of the high school rodeo club, offering cancer support, serving on the Hot Spring County Fair board, and traveling the world to see Nancy and me. Mom volunteered at the Hot Spring County Pioneer Museum and prepared milk can feasts for visiting groups. Dad continued to rodeo until his death. Mom continued to sew, garden, and make jelly and pickles until her eyesight failed. They both were active and involved always—they enjoyed each day every day.

Enjoyment and laughter are also leader's tools. And so, as an ending to this story of stories, we end with one more story, the importance of laughing at yourself—a leadership must.

Linda Stories are famous among my friends and family. These stories are a collection of all of the crazy things that I do, like asking for a Korean brother or designing a Golden Trash Can award. These stories document my impulsiveness, distractibility, my can-do-it attitude. For some reason, I always have to share the details with others. And in doing so, I laugh at myself. I guess I take Will Rogers' advice, *Do the best you can, and don't take life too serious.*

LAUGH AT YOURSELF: A LEADERSHIP MUST

Do the best you can, and don't take life too serious.
—Will Rogers

The first Linda Story took place at the ditch camp. Our mailbox was about half-a-mile from the house, up a dirt lane, over a hill and a railroad track to the old highway. One day, I went to get the mail on my bike. Coming home, the downhill slope and the dried mud ruts in the road got the best of me. My bike hit a rut with speed. I crashed, skinning my knee and hurting my hands.

I yelled out to no one, "BULL SHIT WITH CREAM ON IT!"

I brushed off the dirt and picked up the mail. Slowly I walked my bike home. When I arrived at the gate, I was whimpering. Now I could see blood dripping down my leg. Mom came to my rescue with antiseptic and band-aids. As Mom was doctoring me with her first aid skills, I began to feel better.

Then, as always, my brain began flitting around like a flea. I thought about what I had said up on the hill. My warped, third-grade sense of humor, got the best of me. I forgot about the that swear word.

I blurted out, "Mom, when I crashed, I yelled BULL SHIT WITH CREAM ON IT! Isn't that funny? Bulls shit. But cream comes from the milk cows, not the bulls!"

Mom's face told me that she was not happy with me swearing.

"Linda, you know that you are not to use words like that," she scolded. "Think before you speak. Don't repeat those kinds of words. It isn't what a nice young girl would do." Her face was stern! Her voice was the voice we heard when we were misbehaving.

And then, with a little smile on her face, she continued, "And yes, it is unusual to see cream on bull poop. That would be funny!" She knew that I was at the age that loves knock-knock jokes, too. Third grade humor is weird.

From that day on, I told friends and family about the crazy things I say and do. Then a few years ago, I made a New Year's Resolution to not tell any more "Linda Stories." I would keep the dumb things that I do to myself.

My family and friends said, "No, you can't stop telling us! We love those Linda Stories."

At the same time, many were also saying, "You have to write about your life. You have so many fascinating stories."

Well, to be honest, I didn't want a record of all the dumb things that I've done. So I wrote about two things I love—my memories of Leora's Ranch and my life's study of leadership.

Why do I end this book with a story about bull shit? I want you to laugh and be ready to go forth and do good!

Leaders need to be willing to be human! Leaders need to laugh at themselves when they do silly things. Leaders need to model learning from mistakes and make those mistakes part of the culture of the organization. Life-long learning, correcting the course when needed, and being willing to take risks are all components for leading today. Not all decisions are good ones. Leaders need to know and embrace change when needed. And leaders need to know when to laugh at the process.

My Linda Stories here have shared a leadership philosophy that was developed over a life time of study, practice, and just having fun. I was lucky to have a unique childhood. In examining that remote childhood, I discovered that leadership dispositions were developed.

Leadership dispositions are one's normal behavior, reactions, or responses. In this case, the day-to-day experiences coupled with learning from example and careful observation made leadership something natural to me. There was no formal curriculum or lesson plan. The code of behavior called leadership was passed on through actions, events, personal values, and by example. Dad and Mom did not know how important they were to my leadership development. Mom and Dad were simply making a living and raising a family.

This might be the place to ask you to stop reading stories, and ask you to think of the leadership themes and quotes introduced through my stories. Some of the leadership musts are found in most leadership and management books—1) **seeing the big picture,** 2) **understanding systems,** 3) **handling crisis,** 4) **travel to do the work,** 5) **connecting to the community,** and 6) **building networks.**

Other leadership topics may be found in books that discuss personal traits needed in leaders—1) **learn from mistakes,** 2) **imagine and shape the future,** 3) **be proactive,** 4) **take chances,** 5) **be a lifelong learner,** 6) **laugh at yourself, and** 7) **adapt to an ever-changing world.** Books on leadership of the humanitarian leaders of the world like Ghandi or Martin Luther King include 1) **caring for others,** 2) **developing others,** 3) **paving the way for others,** 4) **respecting humanity,** and 4) **honoring human rights.**

Storytelling and **applied improvisation** are probably not found in many leadership discussions, but are included because they are so much part of my personal leadership style.

I carefully selected these leadership traits because in my experience they encompass effective leadership. All of the leadership dispositions selected and described have served me well in this career that started with being an elementary principal in a district that had just had a month-long teachers' strike. My career ended with leading Media Literacy/Disinformation/Fake News Teachers Training for the U.S. Department of State for central European educators, including Ukrainians. Both offered unique challenges like Dad's first winter with the Blizzard of 1949.

Mom and Dad were perfect leadership trainers. There was no way that they could have purposefully prepared me for the future that I have had. My future work globally was totally outside of their experience. Yet, by example they prepared me not to live at Leora's Ranch, but to embrace life's future.

They believed in me and knew I was ready to meet challenges head on. They gave me confidence and freedom to observe closely, to explore, and to question. What a gift!

And so, with hopes that you will finish the book laughing out loud by yourself, this Leadership Memoir ends with BULL SHIT WITH CREAM on it!

Thanks to my sister, Nancy, the Maxwell bulls at Lewis Park near Red Feathers, Colorado, and a can of Reddi Whip, we also leave you with a picture of it. And if you have a third-grade sense of humor like me, you might even laugh out loud alone at the silliness of it! Especially if you can imagine Nancy and me, now in our 70s, out in the mountain pastures looking for the biggest pile of. . . you know what. (Mom, be proud of me. I didn't say the word!)

For Leadership and Early Childhood
Education Classes or Book Club Discussions

1. The author relates a story about a disappearing way of life in Wyoming sheep ranches. And yet, she makes a case that this background prepared her for future leadership roles in a world far beyond the remote Wyoming ranch. In what ways are we preparing today's children for tomorrow's world? What skills will they need?

2. Robertson tells two stories—her childhood memories on a remote ranch in Wyoming in the 1950s and the adult life leadership stories. She says this is to illustrate that her childhood experiences provided the leadership dispositions that served her well later. Do you agree with her premise? Why or why not?

3. There are many individual stories in this book. What was your favorite? Why? In what way does it help define leadership? Parenting?

4. At the end of each chapter, Robertson asks a question. Did these questions cause you to pause to reflect on your own parenting or leading skills? If yes, why?

5. Were there any surprises in the book? If so, what?

6. For each leadership component, two stories were told—one on the ranch and one from the author's professional life. Which of the two types of stories enhanced your understanding of the leadership component—the early childhood memories or the professional examples?

7. The author wanted to be a rancher, marry a Native American, and raise bulls. How did she get these ideas when she wasn't exposed to any of these aspects of life? What does that tell us about children's creativity and ingenuity?

8. Throughout the book, the author inserted quotes about leadership as a summary of the dispositions highlighted in the chapter's stories. Did reading these quotes make the reader pause and think about the leadership content?

9. Which of the leadership dispositions are the most important for world today?

10. The author gave the book a provocative title. If you could give the book a new title, what would it be?

11. Did you laugh out loud while reading as Robertson suggests?

Acknowledgments

The pandemic of 2020-2021 and shut down, coupled with my retirement at 74, gave me time to think and create. The first year I drafted an academic book on leadership with some stories about growing up in the remote ranch in Wyoming. Like the salons of the Enlightenment in France, I gathered my colleagues and family to share ideas, to read drafts, to provide criticism. Can you believe it? We threw out the first book drafted. I started over. But I did save some of the ideas, photos, and stories to start writing a memoir at Mary Beth Harper's suggestion. Dr. Cathy Hackney and Dr. Averil McClelland, experts in cultural and educational leadership, agreed that a memoir would be a better format. My sister, Nancy Lewis and her husband, Dr. Lon Lewis, read the first manuscript and were more generous as they both had lived the similar childhood on ranches in the west.

In the summer of 2021, I traveled to Wyoming and had conversation with Uncle Carl Schweighart and Aunt Alice Beckley, in their 90s, about ranch life in the 1950s. I visited the Hillberry Ranch and marveled at the modern ranch headquarters. I visited the Hot Springs County Pioneer Museum and Cultural Center and learned that they could help me with old photographs to enrich the story. I came home and started the rewrite in the early fall.

Research began anew by looking at old family photos, pairing stories and events from the Leora Ranch days and educational leadership with similar themes. Conversations with Nancy, cousin Fred Schweighart, and Mary Beth Harper as well as long thoughtful walks in the parks of Geauga County, Ohio, in the winter of 2021-22 helped to shape the book you have just read. Daughter Michelle Settecase tolerated my enthusiastic sharing of each step in the writing process—often while walking with me in the same parks.

For the materials in the stories, I must give thanks to Kent State University and Drs. Joanne and Michael Schwartz, for believing in me in my new role as Director of Gerald H. Read Center for International and Intercultural Education--giving me a wonderful global second career. Gerald H. Read was an innovative leader and serving as the director of the Center in his honor opened the door for me to take chances, be a catalyst for change, and to network around the world. Marion Korllos, Dr. Kenneth Cushner, Olcay Unver, Huseyin Erim, and the Enver Yucel family as well as the U.S. Department of State, USIAD, UNESCO, The Martha Holden Jennings Foundation, IREX, American Councils, and other funding agencies all contributed to the stories told in this book.

As an author, this book was a learning process. Dorrance Publishing read the first manuscript of the memoir, and believed that the story had a wider reader audience than my original thoughts. That was encouraging. Kenzie Saunders was patient and supportive in all of the steps of publishing. Malia Skidmore took family photos and suggestions, and created a fun and engaging cover. Rose Brown and Tom Welsh provided proofreading and editing--both were sorely needed and deeply appreciated.

My deepest appreciation goes to Dad and Mom, Lee and Dot Brunk, for providing the rich family life, living each day with joy and laughter, and embracing learning. Thank you, Mom and Dad, for letting me make mistakes, take chances, and develop a desire to be of service to others. Now I have a memoir to share our combined story with Jackson and Cheyenne—your great grandchildren and my grandchildren—so aptly named after Wyoming cities.

Notice that I used the leadership skills discussed in the process of writing the book—networking with others, travel to do the work, learning from my mistakes, and taking chances. I have loved the process, the connections with people, the investigation of the history of the time, and yes, even the rewriting and editing. Thank you all for your assistance and patience with me.

References

Demming, W. E. Institute. *Quotes from the W. Edward Demming Institute*. Retrieved from http://deming.org/quotes January 10, 2021.

Drah, H. (2021). *24 Groundbreaking Inter-racial Marriage Statistics in 2021*. January 9, 2021. Retrieved from https://2date4love.com/interracial-marriage-statistics/.

Drucker, Peter. (2008). *Good Reads*. Retrieved from https://www.goodreads.com/author/quotes/12008.Peter_F

Foster, W. E. (2019). A Study of the Wyoming Miscegenation Statutes. *Wyoming Law Journal. 10(2,5)* https://scholarship.law.uwyo.edu/cgi/viewcontent.cgi?article=1396&context=wljWyoming Law Journal.

Gardner, H. (2021) Quote from Brainy Quotes. Retrieved from https://www.brainyquote.com/authors/howard-gardner-quotes.

Hackney. C. E. (editor). (2018). *Leading from a Feminist Soul*. Charlette, N.C.: Information Age Publishing.

Harman, B. M. (2020). Why the Best Leaders Laugh in the Face of Failure? Forbes Coaches Council. *Forbes.* January 10, 2020. https://www.forbes.com/sites/forbescoachescouncil/2020/01/10/why-the-best-leaders-laugh-in-the-face-of-failure/?sh=3b2b621c4cb1.

Herbard, G. R. (1995). *Washakie: Sixty Years an Unchallenged Chief.* Lincoln: University of Nebraska Press. p. 23.

Journal of Leadership Education. (2018). Teaching Storytelling as a Leadership Practice. *Association of Leadership Educators.* 17 (1).

Kerr, L. (2000). Recruiting Field Labor. *The Roundup and Ag Roundup* http://www.sweetbeet.com/growernet/news_events/specevents/holly75_sidney/santos.

Kim. E. (2009) The Origins of Korean Adoption: Cold War Geopolitics and Intimate Diplomacy. *US-Korea Institute at SAIS.* (October 1, 2009), https://www.jstor.org/stable/resrep11137?seq=1#metadata_info_tab_contents.

Moore, B. (2017). *Mindsets, Dispositions and Practices of Highly Effective School Leaders.* ERPIC Impact Education Group. (July 7, 2017). https://www.epicimpactedgroup.com/blog/2017/7/7/mindsets-dispositions-and-practices-of-highly-effective-school-leaders.

Morgan. J. (2020). *Thinking Like a Futurist. #1 Skill for Leaders: Here's How to Master it.* Retrieved from https://medium.com/jacob-morgan/thinking-like-a-futurist-is-the-1-skill-for-leaders-heres-how-to-master-it-54cf0c69d3bd (June 25, 2020).

Poole, C., Miller, S. A., Church, E. B. (2021). *How to nurture this important gateway to social and emotional growth, Ages & Stages—Empathy.* New York, NY: Scholastic Inc. Retrieved from https://www.scholastic.com/teachers/articles/teaching-content/ages-stages-empathy/.

Rettig, T. (2017). *Intercultural Empathy: A Guide to Real Understanding Across Cultures*. (November 16, 2017). Retrieved from https://medium.com/intercultural-mindset/intercultural-empathy-a-guide-to-real-understanding-across-cultures-f2f0decbec52.

Rogers, Will. (2021). Will Rogers Memorial Museum Quotes. Retrieved from https://www.willrogers.com/quotes.

Shaw, G. B. (2021). Brainy Quotes from George Bernard Shaw. Retrieved from https://www.brainyquote.com/authors/george-bernard-shaw-quotes.

Sheer, T. J. (2005). *Governor Lady: The Life and Times of Nellie Ross*. Columbia, MO: University of Missouri.

Skarsten, Ugelstad. (2020). Outdoors as an arena for science learning and physical education in kindergarten. *European Early Childhood Education Research Journal*

Tucker, R. (2017). Six Innovation Leadership Skills Everybody Needs to Master. *Forbes.com*. February 9, 2017. Retrieved from https://www.forbes.com/sites/robertbtucker/2017/02/09/six-innovation-leadership-skills-everybody-needs-to-master/?sh=65fc6f655d46

U.S. Department of Agriculture's National Agricultural Statistics Service. (2018) Wyoming Field Office 2018. Retrieved from https://www.nass.usda.gov/Statistics_by_State/Wyoming/Publications/Brochures/Wyoming%20AG%20Profile%20Brochure.pdf.

Tint, B. S., McWaters, V., van Driel, R. (April, 2015) Applied improvisation training for disaster readiness and response: Preparing humanitarian workers and communities for the unexpected. *Journal of Humanitarian Logistics and Supply Chain Management*. 5 (1): 73-94. P. 80f.

Walsh, E. and Walsh D. Van (2019). *How Children Develop Empathy: Smart Parenting, Smarter Kids.* (May 9, 2019). https://www.psychologytoday.com/us/blog/smart-parenting-smarter-kids/201905/how-children-develop-empathy

Warren, M. R. (1920). A Woman Pioneer with the Sheep. *The Saturday Evening Post. May 13, 1920. 8.*

Wetzel, R., Tint, B. (2019). Using Applied Improvisation for Organizational Learning in the Red Cross Red Crescent Climate Centre. In Antonacopoulou, E., Taylor, S.S. (eds.) *Sensuous Learning for Practical Judgement in Professional Practice.* Volume 2: Art-Based Interventions. Cham, Denmark: Cham Springer International Publishing. Pp. 47-74.

Wheatly, M. J. (2009). *Turning to One Another: A Simple Conversation to Restore Hope to the Future.* Oakland, CA: Barrett Koehler Publishers.

Wilen, W. (2005). The Revolution in Kyrgyzstan: A Social Studies Educator's Eyewitness Account". *Social Education*, 69 (4): May/June, 2005, 205-208

Zauche, L. H., Darcy Mahoney, A. E., Thul, T. A., Zauche, M.S., Weldon, A. B., Stepel-Wax, J. L. (2017). *The Power of Language Nutrition of Children's Brain Development, Health and Future Academic Achievement.* Retrieved from: https://www.jpedhc.org/article/S0891-5245(16)30311-X/pdf July/August 2017.

Photos Credits

#1134 *Certificate of Merit* issued by the Holly Sugar Corporation to J. Carmen Quezada Morales,1952, Worland, Wyoming. From Bracero History Archive, Item #3013, http://braceroarchive.org/items/show/3013 (accessed May 8, 2021).

Family Photos from personal archives.

Hopalong Cassidy Pocket Knife Photo. Auction Exchange USA. https://www.mylocal auction.com. Retrieved July 21, 2021.

Hot Spring County Pioneer Museum Photos. (July 2021). Thermopolis, Wyoming. www.thermopolismuseum.com.

Remembering Heart Mountain: Essays on Japanese American Internment in Wyoming, Edited by Mike Mackey, A Western History Book Publication. 1998.

Sheepherder Wagon with Canvas Top. Retrieved from https://www.hansenwheel.com/sheepherder-wagon-with-canvas-top/ on July 21, 2021.

Wrangler Blue Bell Great Moments in Rodeo #2: Bull Riding starring Jim Shoulder of Henryetta, Oklahoma. (1955). Full color, 5-9n x 3.5- in. Retrieved from https://www.mycomicshop.com/search?TID=541331.

Music Quotes Credits

When the Work is Done this Fall. (1893). Songwriter: D. J. O'Malley, 1893. Miles City Stock Growers Journal. Also published in John Lomax's (1910). Cowboy Songs and other Frontier Ballads.

Printed in the USA
CPSIA information can be obtained
at www.ICGtesting.com
JSHW011935251023
50883JS00016B/41